Alpine Level III Study Guide

Alpine Level III Study Guide

Professional Ski Instructors of America Education Foundation

CREDITS

Education Director
Linda J. Crockett

Technical Editor
Weems Westfeldt

Cover Illustration/Design Standards
Lee Reedy Creative

Graphic Design/Pre-press Production
Ken Grasman

Digital Photo Design
Boulder Media Group

Photography
Scott Markewitz

Still Images
Rodnunsky Arts, Ltd.

ISBN 1-882409-11-6

Table of Contents

Acknowledgments

The PSIA Steering Committee developed the concept of presenting the American Teaching System alpine information as an assortment of materials. The pieces of the system manual, study guides, video, and handbook work synergistically to produce a complete picture of an effective alpine lesson.

- The *Alpine Manual* covers the American Teaching System, the role of PSIA in the ski industry, and a variety of subjects that contribute to the working knowledge of ski instruction.
- The study guides available for Level I, II, and III instructors contain the step-by-step procedures for conducting a ski lesson. They are written to be useful for the instructor who teaches, or is preparing for certification, at that level.
- The *Alpine References* video runs parallel to the content in the manual and study guides. It provides moving images of the skiing discussed in the ATS publications and was the source of most of the photos.
- The *Alpine Handbook*—a pocket-sized guide—contains exercises and drills that can be used with any level of class to develop improved learning and skills acquisition.

The study guides were co-authored by David Mannetter and Nancy Oakes of the PSIA Alpine Demonstration Team. These individuals drew upon insights, ideas, and their personal experiences to describe how to present an excellent ski lesson. Reading the study guides is like taking a private lesson with one of these accomplished skiers. David and Nancy set a fine example of teamwork in producing the study guides.

Pat Butowick, ski instructor at Heavenly Ski Resort and technical writer/editor, developed the study questions relating to each chapter of the study guides. She painstakingly distilled the key points to provide a valuable tool for study and discussion. In true PSIA spirit, Pat always provided what was required, plus a little extra.

Weems Westfeldt, a former member of the PSIA Alpine Demonstration Team and currently a trainer with the ski schools of Aspen, served as technical editor for the study guides as well as the manual. Weems worked 25 hours a day to accomplish this task.

Bill Grout, senior executive editor for *SKIING* Magazine, read through the study guides and constantly challenged us to provide technical information in skier-friendly terms.

The PSIA Alpine Demonstration Team developed the core of ideas presented in this edition. The team is instrumental in PSIA's educational process and provides a constant source of creative energy.

The PSIA Board of Directors supported the project both in encouragement and funding.

The review panel for this publication consisted of the following individuals, who offered valuable advice:

Jack Copeland
Johanna Hall
Megan Harvey
Glen Peterson, Ph.D.
Sue Spencer
Calvin Yamamoto

PSIA instructors are also acknowledged, because it is you who can take the words on these pages and transform them into memorable experiences for your students.

Linda J. Crockett
PSIA Education Director

Study Guide Organization

Throughout the beginning and intermediate stages of skiing, the skills the students have developed can be performed through six basic movement patterns:

1. adjusting balance along the length of the skis by pushing the feet forward and pulling them backward,
2. twisting the feet and legs to steer the skis (rotary movements),
3. tipping the feet and legs to engage and release the edges (edge-control movements),
4. moving from foot to foot to transfer weight,
5. flexing and extending legs to control pressure, and
6. using hand and arm movements for balance and pole action.

These basic movement patterns combine to express the four basic skills of skiing: balancing, rotary, edge-control, and pressure-control movements. By combining the movement patterns in different ways, the skier can create the skills needed to handle specific skiing situations.

In Levels 7, 8, and 9, students begin to apply their movements and skills to all-mountain situations and skiing. They learn to make turns that are more dynamic by adjusting to increases in pitch, skiing speed, and more challenging snow conditions. As the situations they encounter on the mountain become more demanding, so must balancing movements become more dynamic.

Similarly, so must students' movements become more powerful and precise. The progressions included in this study guide are intended to help you learn to teach students specific movements and skills to prepare them for skiing the entire mountain.

Unlike the *Level I* and *Level II* study guides, which were arranged by student levels, this study guide is divided into skiing situations—short turns, medium turns, moguls, steeps, powder, crud, and ice. This is the sequence that most students progress through at the upper levels of skiing.

Learning to make more dynamic short turns will open the door for most students to begin to ski moguls, steeps, and off-piste situations. Learning to make more dynamic medium turns gives students the ability to ski groomed snow with less effort and more control. This book assumes that you have acquired the necessary background in teaching styles and class handling techniques while teaching skier Levels 1 through 6.

Use this reference book as you need the information. Its layout is not intended to be followed directly from beginning to end; rather, it is meant to provide you with ideas and options for teaching students at your resort. For this reason, you will find certain progressions in more than one chapter. This redundancy saves you from searching chapter to chapter for a particular exercise.

Be aware that any instructor could just as easily create progressions that develop more toward the edge/pressure side of the spectrum, and when students arrive on

shaped skis, instructors should explore and emphasize those edge/pressure possibilities. You will encounter teaching situations that are not addressed in this book. Consult your ski school trainer to help you fill in any blanks that may exist.

Following each skier level, you will find questions and answers for checking your understanding. Plus, notes pages are interspersed for listing your own progressions and other pertinent information.

The *Alpine Level III Study Guide* corresponds with the *Alpine Manual*. You can refer to the manual whenever you need background information about the Skiing Model, which is the basis for the concepts and progressions in this book. The following list describes where you should look in the manual to find specific information that supports this study guide.

Short Turns: see Chapter 4, The Skiing Model, Levels 7-9, (Dynamic Parallel; Balancing, Rotary, Edge-control, and Pressure-control Movements)
Medium Turns: see Chapter 4, The Skiing Model, Levels 7-9, (Dynamic Parallel; Balancing, Rotary, Edge-control, and Pressure-control Movements)

Note: As you work with any of the materials in the American Teaching System, you may come across unfamiliar ski terminology. Please refer to the glossary and/or text of the *Alpine Manual* for explanation of these concepts. Ski instructors use terms in a variety of ways, so in any technical discussion, always state what you mean and ask others to do the same. While the use of ski terminology is an effective way to communicate with other instructors, you will want to develop non-technical translations of these terms for students.

Short Turns

Lesson Outcome

Students develop short-radius turns by applying the movements learned thus far with increasing quickness and intensity. They learn to blend aggressive, twisting movements of the feet and legs with adequate tipping movements so that skis interact appropriately with the snow. Skiers use flexion and extension movements quickly and accurately to control the rapidly-building pressure that develops during a short-radius turn.

Dynamic Short-radius Turns

In dynamic short-radius turns, the skier's head and upper body are held quietly and face toward the fall line. The stance is flexed to allow quick, powerful twisting and tipping movements of the feet and legs to turn the skis. The turn itself is executed in the space of only a few ski lengths on the snow. The actual distance depends upon the turn shape: in a short, quick turn with a relatively straight shape, or in a pivoted short turn, the distance may be only six to nine feet. In a very round, finished short circumference from the top to the end of the turn the arc of the turn may vary from 12 to 18 feet. The timing and rhythm of the turns is quick and has a minimum of delay between turns. Turns are linked directly from the end of one turn to the initiation of the new turn by immediately tipping and twisting the feet and legs toward the new direction.

Photo 1. Dynamic Parallel Turn

Dynamic short and medium-radius turns share similar physical movements; however, in short turns, the timing and application of the movements quickens and intensifies.

- More countering is required as turns are performed more quickly.
- More aggressive tipping of the legs and feet is necessary to engage or disengage the edges.
- Cadence of pole action and foot-to-foot movements speeds up.
- Flexion and extension of the legs helps to control pressure—both overall pressure and from ski to ski.

There are many variations of short turns: from quick, staccato-like arcs to smooth, round, completed arcs that reach across to the fall line ("reaching short turns").

Short turns are especially suited for:

- steep terrain and narrow slopes with high skier traffic for speed control;
- areas with limited vertical and short runs; and
- bumps. Short turns in the fall line are often the best option for skiing bumps.

Students enjoy mixing dynamic short turns with medium turns. Skiing with a variety of turn shapes promotes versatility and the feeling of getting more for the mileage. A dynamic parallel turn is shown in photo 1.

Many students come to ski school because they want to be able to ski in the fall line and ski the bumps better. This is especially true for students who are progressing from intermediate to advanced terrain. In your lessons, give students the opportunity to first see the movement, then feel it, and finally to understand it. Exercises can be fun and exciting when students understand why the exercises are important and why exercises help them improve. For example, if the students' goal is to improve fall-line skiing so they can ski bumps, try having them ski some

Photo 2. Hip Countering Movements in a Dynamic Parallel

A

B

C

short turns combined with short-turn variations, such as edge-set turns or pivot-slip turns, both of which ultimately help control speed. These short-turn variations will help you learn more about your students and the kind of movements they need to meet their goals and enjoy skiing more.

Improving Stance and Developing Upper and Lower Body "Separation"

To make quick, efficient short turns, students need to be able to "separate" the upper and lower halves of their bodies. This means that the legs and feet move independently of the pelvis and upper body. For the purposes of *this* study guide, "upper body" refers to the head, shoulders, torso, and arms, plus the hips, unless otherwise stated. This is the functional unit that moves independently of the legs, feet, and skis.

If the entire body is turned each time the skis are turned, turn cadence slows and the turns

become cumbersome. If the upper body is held quiet and strong, however, the legs and skis are free to turn much more quickly, accurately, and effortlessly.

Sideslipping in a Corridor

This exercise promotes an efficient, balanced, countered stance (i.e., "open, countered hips"). Hip countering movements are an important component of advanced turns and are shown in photo 2.

The ideal terrain for practicing sideslipping is moderately steep and smoothly groomed. A consistent pitch, without a double fall line or counter-slope, is perfect. Pick a section of the slope that is less crowded, easy to see, and away from skier traffic.

1. Describe the boundaries of an imaginary corridor. The sides of the corridor vary depending on the skill level of the student. For the intermediate student, the corridor should be at least 12

feet wide. For the more advanced and expert student, the corridor should be narrower, with the boundaries being a little more than one ski length wide.

The goal is to slip vertically within the boundaries without skidding forward or backward (toward the right or left side of the trail). Less skilled students will have difficulty staying within the corridor, so for them the goal is simply to experience the sensations rather than perfecting the movements. Students must continually balance themselves over the entire length of the skis to keep them sliding vertically.

2. Pick a distant object directly down the fall line as a target and demonstrate how to aim the upper body toward this object. Although it is nearly impossible to aim the hips directly toward the target, try to come as close as possible, as opposed to facing your hips toward your ski tips. (Women and children tend to achieve this more easily, due to greater hip flexibility).

3. Have your students try what you have just shown them. Have your students practice sideslipping for 60 to 90 feet.
4. Have them change directions and practice slipping in the opposite side, since everyone has a "good" and "bad" side.
5. Have them try making some short turns after this exercise, especially if you run out of suitable terrain. If appropriate terrain is still available, continue with the variations described below.

Note: In order to separate the upper body from the lower body and develop a countered stance while sideslipping, you must twist the torso firmly toward the fall line, stretching the uphill side of the back along the latissimus dorsi muscle. A good range of motion in the hips (made more available by slight flexion in the knee and ankle joints) helps achieve this twisted relationship.

Also, point both shoulders toward the target, reaching with the arms over the downhill ski. This will help create a slight lateral curve and a forward bend in the spine. Maintain a strong upper body with the hips positioned fairly high and over the feet. Avoid exaggerating the bending and curving of the spine as it creates a low, weak stance, characterized by squatting over the tails of the skis.

Open the hips toward the fall line and keep the uphill hip, knee, and foot about half a boot length ahead of the downhill hip, knee, and foot. Lastly, maintain contact between the shin and the tongue of the boot while feeling the bottoms

(ball, arch, and heel) of both feet in order to promote a centered stance.

Variations of Sideslipping in a Corridor: Edge Engagement and Release

Demonstrate these variations and have your students try them.

- Primarily use lower leg movements to tip the skis up on their edges.
- Tip the legs and feet downhill to help bring the upper body more over the feet and skis enabling you to be well-balanced while the skis slip down the corridor. Next, tip the legs and feet in the opposite direction (into the hill).

  This allows you to edge the skis without changing the relationship of the body over the feet. It is important to maintain a countered stance while performing this task to keep a stable upper body.
- After setting your edges, stopping motion, release the skis' edges again by rolling the feet, ankles, and knees toward the fall line.

Have the group add flexion and extension movements to sideslipping. Flexing and extending the legs helps engage and release the ski edges. Demonstrate this exercise in a corridor and have the students try it.

- Release the skis into a vertical sideslip by rolling the feet, ankles, and knees toward the downhill side, while extending the legs.
- Allow the skis to continue slip-

ping while relaxing the legs in this tall, extended attitude.
- Finally, to re-engage the edges, bend the legs by rolling the ankles and knees forward and inward until the skis' edges bite into the snow.

Framing the Target

To provide students with a visual reference, and to give them a means of evaluating their own performance, ask them to hold their poles in front of them and "frame" the target. If the target does not stay centered in the frame of their poles, they will know that they are not holding the upper body in a countered relationship to the lower body.

Balancing Poles

Have your students balance both poles horizontally over their wrists and align them perpendicular to the fall line while sideslipping. If their poles do not remain level with the horizon and downhill of them, students have lost the countered relationship.

Adding Quick, Powerful Turning Movements: Hockey Stops

Sideslipping in a corridor is a good prerequisite for building on the components necessary for hockey stops. Sideslipping develops the centered, countered stance necessary to finish a hockey stop in good balance. Upper and lower body separation or countering movements are enhanced because the legs and feet turn actively against the upper body. Hockey slides and hockey stops are exercises that develop sensations for leg and foot turning movements. Turning the legs and feet against a stable body also creates the sensations of upper and lower body separation and a countered stance.

Begin this exercise on intermediate terrain with a good pitch. The ideal terrain starts with a flatter area, then rolls off into a slightly steeper section. Make sure that the students are not practicing hockey stops in a blind area and that they are visible from above by other skiers.

1. Again, describe the boundaries of an imaginary corridor. Stopping vertically within its boundaries will help your more advanced and expert students refine their skills and balance over their feet.
2. Start by demonstrating how to glide with your skis parallel. It is also a good idea to pick a target. (On steeper terrain, you can start from either a wedge or a bullfighter position [see *Level I Study Guide* for description], then pull your feet into a parallel position).
3. Straight run for about 30 to 60 feet, then turn the skis sideways with the feet going either right or left. This is a quick, pivoting movement of the legs and feet underneath a stable body. The upper body should remain facing down the fall line.
4. Tip the legs and feet back into the hill gradually to come to a stop.
5. Have your students try this

exercise in both directions.
6. Increase the intensity of this exercise by having your students quicken the movements so the skis pivot and stop more quickly. Greater accuracy is required as movements accelerate.

Ask your students to keep the skis parallel while pivoting them. Actively turning the inside leg and foot helps keep the skis from displacing into a christie. Actively turning the inside leg and foot promotes a lead with the inside foot and knee, maintaining an open, countered stance of the hips and upper body. As pivoting begins, more weight is transferred to the outside ski.

The goal for the most refined level of a hockey stop is to stop while maintaining balance and weight over the downhill ski. Reaching with both shoulders over the downhill ski helps center the upper body over the feet and also develops countering with angulation.

Centering and countering the upper body over the feet increases the success of slipping in a vertical line down the fall line. Spraying snow directly down the fall line with the skis' edges is proof that the exercise is being done correctly!

Progression Options: Hockey Stops

- An extremely advanced version of a hockey stop is to perform the exercise on one ski. Try the outside ski; then try the inside ski.
- Add a pole plant to linked hockey stops.

- Try linking pivot slips with the legs flexed to begin the turn. Extend the legs after the ski tips enter the fall line. Add a pole touch.

Linked Hockey Stops

The goal, once again, is to stay somewhat within the boundaries of an imaginary corridor. The confines of the corridor depend on the students' skill level. After having your students try a few hockey stops in both directions, have them practice linking hockey stops together.

1. Make a hockey stop.
2. Once the skis are stopped with edges engaged, the student should be in an angulated position.
3. Release the edges by extending the legs and pointing or twisting knees and ankles toward the new direction. Use the legs and feet to turn both skis into the fall line.
4. Pivot the skis until they point straight down the fall line.
5. Glide in the fall line for a moment, then use the legs and feet to actively turn or pivot the skis out of the fall line to complete the turn.
6. Gradually roll the knees and ankles into the hill, adding resistance to the skis' edges so the skis slow down and stop. This progressive, rolling movement requires some flexion of the ankles and knees. Weight the outside ski by reaching the shoulders down the fall line and over the downhill ski, promoting

Table 1. Comparison Between Pivot Slips and Hockey Stops

Pivot Slips	Hockey Stops
Skis continue to slip throughout the maneuver (More consistent speed)	Skis slow and then stop
You flex directly over the skis to allow them to continue to slip down the hill	You roll the ankles and knees to edge the skis (and bring them to a stop)
More equal weight between both feet	Mostly outside-leg dominant

good angulation.

7. Extend the legs again and change directions. Extending the legs unweights and releases the skis so they can turn in the fall line. A wind-up movement is created when the upper body is twisted against the lower body and vice versa.

Unweighting the skis by extending the legs allows the body to unwind and promotes quicker leg and foot turning movements as long as the upper body is held facing downhill (through muscular effort).

Pivot Slips

Emphasize turning both legs and both feet. Keep the upper body centered and facing down the hill. A centered, countered upper body promotes a balanced stance with even weight distribution over the entire length of the skis. A balanced stance allows the student to stay within the corridor's boundaries.

Have your students add a pole swing while flexing, and a pole plant while pivoting the skis to enhance timing and balance, and anchor the upper body in the

countered relationship. Give students enough time to practice so that they can learn both the movements and the proper timing. A comparison between pivot slips and hockey stops is shown in Table 1.

Moving from Pivot Slips into Short-radius Turns

This progression helps students to move from pivot slips to short-radius turns.

1. Pivot the skis.
2. After the skis begin to slip laterally down the corridor, roll the knees and ankles into the hill to engage edges. Rather than increasing this rolling action to bring the skis to a stop, press the shins into the boot tongues while tipping the feet into the hill to keep the skis moving forward and across the hill as the edges begin to bite.
3. Remain flexed and allow the skis to carry you across the hill a short distance while swinging the pole tip forward.
4. Plant the pole in conjunction with an extension movement to release the edges.

5. At the same time, pivot both feet and skis in the opposite direction and allow the skis to slip laterally down the hill.
6. Re-engage the edges progressively to once again get the skis to track back across the hill.
7. Repeat this sequence of movements several times.
8. After the group can comfortably execute the movements in the described sequence, ask them to tip their skis onto the new set of edges much sooner while maintaining the same level of power in the twisting (pivoting) movements.

Remaining flexed while twisting and tipping the skis in the opposite direction helps both actions.

9. After linking 15 or 20 turns with this movement combination, slow the rate of pivoting slightly to lengthen the shape of the turn. Throughout this progression, as soon as you have planted one pole, you should begin to swing the other pole for the next pole plant.

This progression should help students understand both the sequence of movements and the timing necessary to make linked short turns. To further develop both their understanding and skill base, you can introduce the following variations.

Edge-set Turns

Edge-set turns are a refinement of linked hockey stops. Quicken the pace of linking the hockey stops. Instead of gradually rolling and engaging the edges of the skis to a stop, make this movement of the ankles and feet a snappy, staccato action. Add a pole plant with the edge-set. The sensations of speeding and then slowing are a feature of hockey stops, linked hockey stops, and edge-set turns. The students will also sense that they are adding energy to the skis and to the turn and that this extra force rebounds them slightly into the next turn.

Edge-set turns are also called check turns, appropriately named because they check or brake the skier's speed. The shape that the ski makes on the snow resembles a check motif, with a flatter or straighter shape at the end of the arc.

Variation of Edge-set Turns: Spraying Snow at the Bottom of the Turn

Practice short, edge-set turns while trying to spray snow directly down the fall line at the bottom of the turn arc. Add a pole plant with the edge-set. Skiing on intermediate to advanced terrain with a steep pitch helps in performing this exercise and spraying snow. Showing the

bases of the skis to a distant landmark down the fall line is also a good exercise.

Variation of Edge-set Turns: Spraying Snow at the Middle of the Turn

Practice short, edge-set turns while de-emphasizing the pole plant. Try to spray the snow to the side of the arc while the skis are in the fall line. If there are trees on the side of the slope, try to spray the snow or show the bases of the skis toward the trees.

Short-swing Turns

Make short-swing turns by quickening the timing of the edge-set turns where the snow sprays at the bottom or the top of the turn. This type of turn is very quick and is effectively applied when skiing small, narrow moguls.

More Demanding Exercise Lines

In some cases, you may wish to take a more athletic approach with your exercise lines. This is especially true if you are working with young students or with students who wish to ski steep terrain as soon as possible. Let the fitness levels and athletic abilities of the group determine whether you incorporate these options into your lesson. Use these options sparingly because they are so demanding.

Hop Turns

Practicing sideslipping and pivot

slips in a corridor will give students the edge control and twisting or pivoting movements they need for a short turn. To increase the level of challenge and help anchor movements already learned, have them try hop turns. This is intense exercise for even the most adept student.

Hop turns require an explosive turning movement of both legs and both feet to change the direction of the skis, and stance and balancing movements are crucial. After the upper and lower body twist against one another and the edges are released through unweighting, the body tends to unwind as it realigns itself. When you anchor the upper body by a solid pole plant, the lower body tends to unwind toward the upper body. This unwinding effect, when executed from a balanced stance, enhances the leg turning movements.

1. With skis parallel and across the hill, target the hips and upper body down the fall line. Maintain rounded shoulders and a curved spine to help keep the upper body aligned over the feet. Stand flexed with both ankles and knees pressed forward and tipped into the hill and with strong contact over the arches. Focus the majority of weight on the downhill ski.
2. Plant the downhill pole solidly in the snow.
3. Hop off the snow by extending the ankles and knees explosively, leaving the pole tip in the snow.
4. Twist the feet and legs while in the air, pivoting the skis around the pivot point (or axis) of the boots.

5. Flex again and plant the other pole upon landing to prepare to hop and twist the feet and skis the other way.

6. Practice with a few seconds between hops initially, then begin to link the hop turns without hesitation. Hop turns primarily depend on leg and foot movements.

Pole use also offers important contributions:

- timing,
- deflection,
- stabilizing the upper body,
- providing a point of contact with the snow,
- enhancing balance,
- anchoring the countered relationship between the upper and lower body, and
- propelling you off the ground (by pushing your arm and hand against the pole grip).

Edge-wedge Hops

If you want a more challenging variation of hop turns to improve students' versatility or reinforce edge control and foot-to-foot movements, you can teach edge-wedge hops. Begin on a moderate pitch.

1. Maintain a countered relationship between the upper and lower body.

2. Position the skis in a wedge facing down the fall line. Feel strong contact over the arches and inner sides of both feet to help control the inside edges of both skis. Also, feel the shins touch firmly against the boot

tongues to ensure a more centered position of the hips, and therefore the upper body, over the feet.

3. Lift one foot off the snow as you begin to glide forward and hop onto it.

4. Make small, lateral hops from edge to edge while moving straight down the fall line.

   The foot, and primarily the ankle, dominate the movements. Extend from the ankle to jump from the old edge and flex the ankle to engage the new edge. Contact progressively increases forward and against the inside of the boot tongue as the ankle flexes. The upper body stays relatively quiet, as you displace your weight from edge to edge, while leaping from foot to foot (more specifically, from arch to arch).

5. Plant the right pole when hopping from right to left, and plant the left pole when hopping from left to right.

   Pole action can help with both timing the hop and stabilizing the upper body. Firmly planting the pole blocks and temporarily halts the forward momentum, allowing the skier to jump off the old edge and onto the new edge. Pole plant action eventually lightens to a touch, as students' skills develop and sense of balance improves. However, ankle movements, not pole actions, develop and control the way the hips and upper body are centered over the feet. At this point, students will certainly have the component movements

and skills they need to link short-radius turns. It will be easiest if they start with short, quick turns that require a high degree of pivoting. In this scenario, students control their speed by setting the edges to increase friction and reduce forward glide.

Technical Aspects of Skill Development

Balancing and Stance Movements

A fairly tall stance with a slight bend in the ankles, knees, hips, and spine provides greater muscular and skeletal use of the body. The hips and torso must be centered over the feet and skis for other skills to be implemented effectively. A skier continually moves in and out of balance while skiing. To maintain dynamic balance, the skier must continuously make lateral, vertical, and fore/aft adjustments within each turn and from turn to turn.

Linking short-radius turns and maintaining dynamic balance depends on the successful execution of the basic skills. Focusing on different attitudes of the body helps the skier maintain a range of dynamic balancing movements. A countered stance allows for such a range of balancing movements and is extremely important in skiing short turns. This is created when the upper body points down the fall line, twisting against the lower body. Targeting the upper body down the fall line and aiming the torso in a different direction from the skis helps upper and lower body separation.

Completing a ski turn requires turning the legs and feet underneath a fixed, stable upper body and is a countering movement. Rounding out the shoulders, curving the spine, and holding the poles in peripheral view are all helpful in maintaining a stable upper body and creating a countered stance. This focus allows the skier to balance around his or her center of mass which also helps align the upper body over the feet.

Distributing weight equally around the feet allows versatile, dynamic balancing movements. Good balancing movements are enhanced by feeling strong contact over the downhill arch and feeling the shin of the downhill leg press forward and to the inside of the tongue of the boot (along the tibialis anterior muscle). Feeling these contact points aligns the skier's weight over the inside edge of the downhill ski. A small bit of pressure to the uphill or outside edge of the uphill ski is enhanced by slightly pressing the shin forward and to the outside of this boot (along the peroneus longus muscle). Basically, the skier should feel 85 to 95 percent of his or her weight distributed over the outside/downhill ski, with the remainder distributed over the uphill edge of the inside or uphill ski near the tip.

Combining the weight distribution with countering action of the upper body creates a consequent lead of the uphill foot, leg, hip, shoulder, and arm. Although it is nearly impossible to point the hips directly down the fall line, these actions keep the hips open and pointing closer toward the upcoming turn. (Women and children tend to achieve this more readily as they are slightly more flexible in the hips.) Aligning the hip and keeping it open and countered is important for maintaining correct balancing movements. The hips and torso essentially face directly down the fall line in a very quick short-swing or short-radius turn. The hips move off the target and toward the apex of the upcoming turn with a rounder, more reaching turn across the fall line.

Rotary Movements

Turning the legs and feet so that the skis change directions is a simple rotary movement. Skiing short turns requires both quick leg and foot turning movements and unweighting movement (pressure-control movements) which are necessary for stopping and starting the turn. Countering movements or skiing through a countered position are important components of short turns and are by-products of counter-rotation, another rotary movement.

A countered position is static and is created when the hips and torso rotate down the fall line or toward the intended turn, while the lower body remains fixed. Sideslipping in a corridor is an exercise which encourages a countered stance or position. The upper body faces downhill while the skis point across the slope or fall line in a secure parallel position. The process of rotating the upper body against a fixed lower body relates directly to stance and balancing movements.

Once the skier is moving, a countering movement occurs (by turning the lower body against a stable and fixed upper body). Hockey stops help generate the action of turning the legs against the stable upper body. Staying within a corridor refines this action as legs turn precisely underneath rock-solid hips and upper body.

Practicing linked hockey stops or pivot sideslips combines turning the legs and feet with unweighting actions of the skis. Unweighting occurs through leg flexion or extension, as well as tipping the legs and feet laterally, which directly relates to edge-control movements.

Note: Counter-rotation is a movement which occurs as the upper body twists against the lower body. The body then uncoils like a spring. Counter-rotation in skiing often puts the skier in an unbalanced position. Plus, unwinding a twisted body requires strong unweighting. However, many times when we ski into an unbalanced attitude, a counter-rotation movement helps us regain a countered, balanced position.

Edge-control Movements

Engaging and releasing the skis' edges are edge-control movements. Tipping the legs and feet helps engage and release the edges from one turn to the next. How the edges of the skis interact with the snow's surface and the degree of tipping are also edging movements. Edging movements are directly related to the lateral movements of dynamic balance.

Usually, when the skis are tipped onto the edges, with the skier balancing on or against them, the skis and feet are aligned away from the body. The skier's hips and upper body are still centered over the feet, even though the skis and feet are away from the body. This action occurs when the skier is skiing in dynamic balance.

Balancing around the center of mass also allows the skier to balance over the edge of the outside/downhill ski. When the skier is balanced, the feet and legs are able to fine-tune the edging movements by increasing and decreasing the skis' edge angle. These balancing and edging movements are called angulation.

The tipping action of the skis begins with the lower legs and feet. The skis' edges are released first by lightening the downhill ski so that the student's weight moves momentarily to both skis. As the skis are released into the turn, the outside foot everts and pronates inside the ski boot.

The ski boot is constructed of rigid material and therefore transfers the tipping action to the ski. The pronating and everting movements of the foot are accompanied by inward femoral rotation. These actions of the legs and feet promote the crossing-over of the hips and upper body toward the inside of the turn when hips are correctly aligned over the feet.

Edging movements of the inside leg and foot mirror those of the outside leg, although the mechani-cal functions are reversed. The inside foot supinates and inverts causing an outward femoral rotation. Again, with the rigidity of boots, this makes the ski release from its previously engaged edge.

Accomplishing this action requires the student to feel strong contact on the outer side of the foot inside the boot. Because there is slight inward and outward rotation of the legs, edging movements overlap with rotary movements. When the body is centered and relaxed in an aligned stance, the action of the legs allows the hips and upper body to cross-over the feet and legs.

Sideslipping in a corridor, while releasing and engaging the edges, is a good sensory exercise for developing edging movements. The skis are released and engaged by rolling ankles and knees underneath a centered, stable upper body. Hockey stops promote the development of edge engagement as knees and ankles gradually roll into the hill and tip skis onto their edges for slowing and stopping.

Linking hockey stops heightens the sensations of edge release as knees and ankles roll or point down the hill. This action of the legs allows the upper body to cross-over the skis in the direction of the new turn. Edge-wedge hops help develop the sensations of proper form and body movements and also polish edge engagement.

Pressure-control Movements

Distributing weight evenly fore and aft over the entire length of the skis is a pressure-control move-ment related to fore/aft balancing. Unweighting the skis and transferring weight from ski to ski are also pressure-control movements. Unweighting the skis is accomplished by both foot-to-foot and leg movements. The legs move up, down, and laterally, to unweight the skis and absorb both uneven terrain and the forces generated in a turn.

Foot-to-foot movements are pressure-control movements related to the lateral movements of dynamic balancing. How students stand on their skis affects fore/aft balancing movements and all subsequent movements. Feeling the bottom of the foot (ball, arch, and heel) throughout a turn is good feedback for even weight distribution over the ski in a short turn.

The timing and intensity of short turn movements quickens, so feeling only the arch is also appropriate for maintaining even weight distribution. Feeling strong contact of the outside or downhill shin against the inner side of the tongue of the boot is a positive sensation for maintaining pressure over the corresponding arch. These sensations promote good balancing and pressuring movements over the skis.

Extension and flexion, as well as lateral movements of the legs, unweight the skis, which is necessary for turning and changing directions. The student has unlimited options for this unweighting movement.

For the sake of adaptability, versatility, and continued improvement, it is important that the student use a range of leg movements. Sideslipping, hockey stops, edge-wedge hops, and hop turns all contribute to proper weight distribution movements, both fore and aft, and from foot to foot.

As a student's skills develop, balancing solely and evenly on the inside edge of the outside/downhill ski is ultimately the goal. Practicing hockey stops and sideslipping while staying in a corridor promotes even fore/aft pressure and balancing movements. In fact, performing any kind of hop turn is nearly impossible without proficient fore/aft balancing and pressure movements.

Edge-wedge hops are perfect for developing edging movements. These, along with practicing hockey stops and sideslipping while focusing pressure on the downhill ski, also enhance foot-to-foot movements.

Unweighting, through extension and flexion, is enhanced by practicing sideslipping, hockey stops, any hop turn variations, or absorption turns. The legs flex and extend in any of these tasks.

The important point is that the legs are constantly moving and are never locked into position. As students advance, they appropriately apply extension and flexion, as terrain and snow conditions demand.

Increased awareness and application of both tipping and turning movements promote unweighting. The action of tipping and turning the legs allows the upper body to simply move across the skis, thereby unweighting the skis.

Questions: Short Turns

1. List the six basic movement patterns of skiing.

    1 fore/aft   2 Turning (Rotary)
    3 lateral
    4 foot to foot
    5 extension/flexion

    6 Pole action

2. Choose one or more of the following:
    Compared to medium and long-radius turns, short turns involve:
    A.   Fewer tipping movements
    B.   Less countering
    C.   More turning movements
    D.   More rapid foot-to-foot movements

3. Choose one or more of the following:
    Short turns are especially suited for:
    A.   Areas with limited vertical and short runs
    B.   Fall-line turns in the bumps
    C.   Skiing at the end of the day when your legs are tired
    D.   Speed control for steep terrain and narrow slopes with high skier traffic

4. Choose the best answer:
    Which of the following helps control pressure in short turns:
    A.   Flexing only
    B.   Extending only
    C.   Both flexing and extending

5. For short turns, what should you do with your upper body to allow your legs and skis
    to turn more quickly and effortlessly?

    Counter-Rotate   Keeping the upper body quiet & strong

6. The study guide suggests having your students try to sideslip vertically within an imaginary corridor. About how wide should this corridor be for your more advanced and expert students?

½ ski length either side, corridor (no more then 1 ski length total)

7. Choose the best answer:
In a sideslip, in order to separate the upper body from the lower body and to develop a countered stance, twist the torso firmly toward the fall line, stretching the:
A. Gastrocnemius muscle
B. Latissimus dorsi muscle
C. Transversalis muscle
D. Vastus lateralis muscle

8. True or false:
Slightly flexing in the ankles and knees helps you achieve a better range of motion in your hips.

9. When sideslipping within a corridor, what does the study guide suggest your students do with their shoulders and arms?

Point the shoulders down the hill toward a target down the fall line & keep the arms reaching forward over the downhill ski

10. Choose one or more of the following:
In a vertical sideslip:
A. Slightly exaggerate the bend and curve of the spine
B. Maintain contact between the shin and the tongue of the boot
C. Feel the ball, arch, and heel of each foot
D. Face toward your ski tips

11. Circle the best choice:
In the sideslipping edge-engagement and release exercise, after sideslipping you primarily use lower leg movements to tip the skis up on their edges. As a result, (the feet move out from under the body) / (the relationship between the feet and the body will remain unchanged).

12. Fill in the blanks:
Adding extending and flexing to the sideslipping exercise helps: _to release_ and _engage_ the edges.

13. What can you add to the sideslip exercise to help your students determine if they are holding their upper body in a countered relationship to their lower body?

Slipping in a corridor
(frame)
Spotting a target down the fall line
Laying the poles horizontally across the wrists

14. Choose one or more of the following:
    For steeper terrain, the study guide suggests starting the hockey stop exercise:
    A. From a wedge
    B. From a bullfighter position
    C. With your skis perpendicular to the fall line

15. Choose one or more of the following:
    Actively turning your inside leg and foot while pivoting your skis sideways in a hockey stop helps:
    A. Promote a lead with the inside foot and knee
    B. Maintain openness of the hips and upper body
    C. Keep the skis from stemming

16. Choose the best answer:
    Which of the following proves that a student is doing the hockey stop exercise correctly?
    A. Spraying snow perpendicular to the fall line
    B. Spraying snow directly uphill
    C. Spraying snow directly down the fall line

17. The study guide gives four progression options for the hockey stop. Name two of these.

    Pole plant to linked Hockey stop

    Hockey stops on one ski (outside, then inside ski)

18. Choose one or more of the following:
    For hockey stops, reaching with your shoulders down the fall line and over the downhill ski:
    A. Results in maximum braking from the uphill ski
    B. Weights the downhill ski
    C. Promotes an angulated body position
    D. Helps center the body over the feet

19. Fill in the blanks:
    Which of the following statements describes linked pivot slips and which describe hockey stops:
    A. Skis slow and then stop

    _HS_

    B. Skis continue to slip throughout the maneuver

    _P.S._

    C. You flex directly over the skis to allow them to continue to slip down the hill

    _PS_

    D. Mostly outside-leg dominant

    _HS_

20. In the pivot slips in a corridor exercise, what should students do to enhance timing and balance and anchor the upper body in a countered relationship to the lower body?

Use Pole Swing / pole plants as pivot happens
(while flexing)

21. Another name for edge-set turns is:

Check turns

22. True or (false): *No "ankle movements"?*
In edge-wedge hops, using the poles correctly develops and controls the way the hips and upper body are centered over the feet.

23. Circle the best choice:
Hop turns primarily depend upon (leg and foot movements) / (pole use).

24. The study guide lists a number of uses for poles in hop turns. Name three of these.

Stabalizing the upper body
Timing
deflecting

25. Circle the best choice:
In edge-wedge hops, plant the (left) / (right) pole when hopping from the right to the left foot.

26. True or (false): *"Extending"*
In linked hockey stops, unweighting the skis by retracting the legs allows the body to unwind and promotes quicker leg and foot turning movements, as long as you use muscular effort to hold your upper body facing downhill.

27. True or (false): *"Taller" & slight*
An athletic stance with a pronounced bend in the ankles, knees, hips, and spine provides greater muscular and skeletal use of the body.

28. ((True) or false:
Rounding out the shoulders, curving the spine, and holding the poles in peripheral view are all helpful in maintaining a stable upper body and creating a countered stance.

29.   Choose one or more of the following:
       The hips face toward the apex of the upcoming turn in:
       A.   A very quick short-swing
       B.   Quicker short-radius turns
       C.   Rounder and more reaching turns across the fall line

30.   Choose one or more of the following:
       To align your weight over the inside edge of the downhill ski, feel:
       A.   Strong contact over the downhill arch
       B.   The shin of the downhill leg press along the peroneus longus muscle
       C.   The shin of the downhill leg press along the tibialis anterior muscle

31.   Choose the best answer:
       Separating or turning the lower body below a stable upper body is called a:
       A.   Countered position
       B.   Countering movement
       C.   Counter-rotation movement

32.   Choose one or more of the following:
       Which of the following exercises involves a countering movement?
       A.   Sideslipping in a corridor
       B.   Hockey stops
       C.   Pivot sideslips

33.   Circle the best choice:
       As the skis are released into a turn, the outside foot:
       A.   Pronates and everts
       B.   Pronates and inverts
       C.   Supinates and everts
       D.   Supinates and inverts

34.   Choose one or more of the following:
       Distributing weight evenly fore and aft over the entire length of the skis is:
       A.   A balancing movement
       B.   A rotary movement
       C.   An edging movement
       D.   A pressure-control movement

35.   True or false:
       In the sideslipping exercise, the legs are constantly moving and are never stuck or locked in one position.

36.   True or false:
       Using a countering action and keeping most of your weight over the downhill ski will create
       a consequent lead of the uphill foot, leg, hip, shoulder, and arm.

Answers: Short Turns

1. The six basic movement patterns of skiing are:
   1) Adjusting balance along the length of the skis by pushing the feet forward and pulling them backward
   2) Twisting the feet and legs to steer the skis (rotary movements)
   3) Tipping the feet and legs to engage and release the edges (edge-control movements)
   4) Moving from foot to foot to transfer weight
   5) Flexing and extending legs to control pressure
   6) Using hand and arm movements for balance and pole usage

2. C & D. In short turns, the action of turning the legs and feet increases and the cadence of foot-to-foot movements quickens. Additionally, both tipping movements and the degree of countering increase.

3. A, B, & D. Short turns are suited for areas with limited vertical and short runs, fall line turns in bumps, and steep terrain with narrow slopes and high skier traffic.

4. C. *Flexing and extending*. Both flexing and extending movements help control pressure in short turns.

5. Holding the upper body *quiet and strong* in a short-radius turn allows the legs and skis to turn much more quickly and effortlessly.

6. *One ski length wide*. For the more advanced and expert student, the corridor for a vertical sideslip should be little more than one ski length wide.

7. B. In order to separate the upper body from the lower body and develop a countered stance, twist the torso firmly toward the fall line, stretching the uphill side of the back along the *latissimus dorsi muscle*.

8. *True*. A good range of motion in the hips is made more available by a slight flexion in the knee and ankle joints and will help you twist your torso toward the fall line.

9. *Point both shoulders toward a target directly down the fall line and reach with the arms over the downhill ski*. For sideslipping in a corridor, the study guide suggests having your students point both shoulders toward a target and reach with the arms over the downhill ski to help create a slight lateral curve and forward bend in the spine.

10. B & C. In a vertical sideslip, *maintain contact between the shin and the tongue of the boot while feeling the ball, arch, and heel of each foot* in order to promote a centered stance. Avoid exaggerating the bend and curve of the spine, as it creates a low, weak stance characterized by squatting over the tail of the ski. The hips should be fairly high and over the feet. Although it is nearly impossible to point the hips at a target that is directly down the fall line, try to come as close as possible, as opposed to facing toward your ski tips. (Women and children tend to be more flexible in the hip area.)

11. *The relationship between the feet and body will remain unchanged*. By primarily using lower leg movements to tip the skis onto their edges, you should be able to edge the skis without changing the relationship of the body over the feet. It is important to maintain a countered stance while performing this task to keep the upper body stable.

12. *Release and engage*. Extending and flexing the legs during the sideslip and release exercise helps release and engage the skis' edges.

13. *Frame a target or balance the poles horizontally over the wrists.*

    Framing a target: To provide students with a visual reference, and to give them a means of evaluating their own performance in the sideslip stops, you could ask them to hold the poles in the middle and frame a downhill target. If the target does not stay centered in the frame of their poles, they will know that they are not holding the upper body in a countered relationship to the lower body.

    Balancing poles: You could also have your students balance both poles horizontally over the wrists and align them perpendicular to the fall line while sideslipping. If their poles do not remain level with the horizon and down the hill from them, the students have lost the countered relationship.

14. A & B. On steeper terrain, you can start the hockey stop exercise *from a wedge or a bullfighter position*, then pull your feet parallel.

15. A, B, & C. Actively turning the inside leg and foot will help *keep the skis from displacing into a stem relationship* when pivoting them sideways in a hockey stop, and will *promote a lead with the inside foot and knee, maintaining openness and countering of the hips and upper body*.

16. C. Spraying snow directly down the fall line with the skis' edges proves that the hockey stop exercise is being done correctly.

17. Progression options for hockey stops:
    1) A more advanced option for hockey stops is to maintain a flexed position with the legs while unweighting and releasing the skis' edges to stop.
    2) An extremely advanced version of a hockey stop is to perform the exercise on one ski. Try the outside ski. Then try the inside ski.
    3) Add a pole plant to linked hockey stops.
    4) Try linking pivot slips with the legs flexed to begin the turn. Extend the legs after the ski tips enter the fall line. Add a pole touch.

18. B, C, & D. For hockey stops, weighting the outside ski by reaching with your shoulders down the fall line and over the downhill ski promotes an angulated body position. Reaching with both shoulders over the downhill ski helps center the upper body over the feet and also puts you in an angulated position.

19. A= Hockey stops, B= Linked pivot slips, C= Linked pivot slips, D= Hockey stops
    A. In hockey stops, skis slow and then stop.
    B. In linked pivot slips, skis continue to slip throughout the maneuver.
    C. In linked pivot slips, you flex directly over the skis to allow them to continue to slip down the hill. (In hockey stops, you roll the ankles and knees to edge the skis and bring them to a stop.)
    D. Hockey stops are mostly outside-leg dominant. (In linked pivot slips, the weight is distributed more equally between both feet.)

20. *A pole plant.* In the pivot slips in a corridor exercise, having your students add a pole swing while flexing and a pole plant as they pivot the skis will enhance timing and balance and will also anchor the upper body in a countered relationship to the lower body.

21. *Check turns.* Edge-set turns are also called check turns, appropriately named because they check or brake the skier's speed.

22. *False. Ankle movements*, and not pole actions, develop and control the way the hips and upper body are centered over the feet.

23. *Leg and foot movement.* Hop turns primarily depend upon leg and foot movements.

24. *Timing, deflecting, stabilizing the upper body, enhancing balance by providing a point of contact with the snow, anchoring the countered relationship of the upper and lower body, and getting you off the ground.* In hop turns, you use your poles for timing, deflecting, stabilizing the upper body, enhancing balance by providing a point of contact with the snow, anchoring the countered relationship of the upper and lower body, and getting you off the ground. (You do this by pushing your hand and arm against the pole grip.)

25. *Right.* In edge-wedge hops, plant the *right* pole when hopping from the right to the left foot, and plant the *left* pole when hopping from the left to the right foot.

26. *False.* Unweighting the skis by *extending* the legs allows the body to unwind and promotes quicker leg and foot turning movements as long as the upper body is held facing downhill (through muscular effort).

27. *False.* A *fairly tall* stance with a *slight* bend in the ankles, knees, hips, and spine provides greater muscular and skeletal use of the body.

28. *True.* Rounding out the shoulders, curving the spine, and holding the poles in peripheral view are all helpful in maintaining a stable upper body and creating a countered stance.

29. C. Essentially, the hips and torso face directly down the fall line in a very quick short-swing or short-radius turn. The hips move off the target and toward the apex of the upcoming turn with a *rounder and more reaching turn across the fall line.*

30. A & C. Good balancing movements are enhanced by feeling *strong contact over the downhill arch* and feeling the *shin of the downhill leg* press forward and to the inside of the tongue of the boot (*along the tibialis anterior muscle*). Feeling these contact points aligns the skier's weight over the inside edge of the downhill ski. A small bit of pressure to the uphill or outside edge of the uphill ski is enhanced by slightly pressing the shin forward and to the outside of this boot (along the muscle).

31.　B. *Countering movement.* Separating or turning the lower body below a stable upper body is called a *countering movement.* This focus allows the skier to balance around his or her center of mass which also helps align the upper body over the feet.

A *countered position* is static and is created when the hips and torso rotate down the fall line or toward the intended turn, while the lower body remains fixed.

Counter-rotation is a movement which occurs as the upper body twists against the lower body in the opposite direction. The body then acts like a spring and uncoils.

32.　B & C. Once the skier is moving, a *countering movement* occurs by turning the lower body against a stable and fixed upper body. *Hockey stops* help generate the action of turning the legs against a stable upper body. *Pivot sideslips* combine turning the legs and feet with unweighting actions so that the skis turn. Sideslipping in a corridor is an exercise which encourages a *countered stance or position.* The upper body faces downhill while the skis point across the slope or fall line in a secure parallel position.

33.　A. As the skis are released into a turn, the outside foot *pronates and everts* inside the ski boot. The inside foot supinates and inverts. The ski boot is constructed with a rigid material, and therefore transfers the tipping action to the ski.

34.　A & D. Distributing weight evenly fore and aft over the entire length of the skis is a *pressure-control movement* and is related to fore and aft *balancing.*

35.　*True.* In sideslipping, as well as in the other tasks and exercises, the legs are constantly moving and are never stuck or locked in one position.

36.　*True.* Combining a countering action with keeping most of your weight over the downhill ski creates a consequent lead of the uphill foot, leg, hip, shoulder, and arm.

Notes

Medium Turns

Lesson Outcome

Students learn to apply appropriate combinations of the fundamental skills to link medium-radius turns with strong balance, solid angulation, and confident skill blends. The basic patterns begin with balancing movements and then work toward edging movements through tipping the legs and feet. Students develop twisting movements to steer the skis appropriately, and flexion and extension movements to control pressure on the skis. Movement from foot to foot is also enhanced and combined with the rest of the basic movement patterns.

Becoming an all-mountain skier challenges the student to ski a variety of turn shapes from short to medium to long. Medium-radius turns are appropriate for a wide variety of situations and types of terrain: they are a viable option for skiing groomed terrain, especially if the hill is not too steep. The cadence is slower and less fatiguing than that of short turns; therefore, they could be a better alternative for skiing at the end of the day when your legs are tired. They are good for exploring the movements necessary to develop carved turns. The slower cadence of a medium turn allows you more time to experience and feel the different movements as you execute them.

As students refine the movements described in the following progressions, they are able to link all of their turns more accurately so that they begin to ski from arc to arc. They ultimately apply their movements without interruption or pause. The technical goal of every good skier is to keep the body moving with the skis as they carve from arc to arc.

The following progressions and exercises help develop and refine the technique for skiing medium turns. They also help anchor the sensations of upper-level skiing.

Balancing Movements

Balancing movements are crucial to linking medium turns. Essentially, there is no such thing as a balanced "position," because skiing is a process of moving with gravity down a slope. Skiers continuously move up and down, from side to side, and fore and aft to maintain dynamic balance. See photo 3 for an example of stance that displays good fore/aft balance. The hip acts as a universal joint, integrating movements of the upper and lower body to maintain balance. Coordinating the upper and lower body through this central joint allows a centered stance with a stable torso and freedom of movement of the legs.

For proper upper body posture:

- stand with a slightly curved spine and relaxed, rounded arms and shoulders;
- hold your hands in front of your torso and hips at approximately rib-cage height; and
- keep all your joints slightly bent.

To promote a centered stance, you should feel your shins in soft

Photo 3. Fore/Aft Balance in Dynamic Parallel Turning

contact with the boot tongues while standing in a neutral position. Focusing on "relaxing tall" is a good way to keep your body in balance. The body must compensate to maintain balance if you flex too much at the hips or ankles and hang in the front of the boot. Essentially, it is the feet, rather than equipment, supporting your weight.

The exercises described in this section develop the sensation of balancing while moving down the hill, rather than balancing against the equipment (skis and boots). The legs and feet work up and down, fore and aft, and side to side underneath the upper body. These continuous movements of the legs keep the body moving slightly ahead of the feet and promote centering and re-centering to maintain dynamic balance.

After you have introduced an exercise and given your students a chance to practice it, you should incorporate the movements into a skiing sequence. This helps bridge the gap between the exercise and its application to real skiing situations. If a variety of snow conditions exist and time allows, you should also try to apply the newly-developed movements to as many snow and terrain conditions as possible.

Traversing

Even though there is little to no traversing in linked medium turns, traversing exercises enhance and develop balance (both lateral and fore/aft), and tipping movements (to edge the skis). Traversing is an essential skill for upper-level students if for no other reason than it gives them an additional way of moving around on the mountain. When teaching the following exercise, keep in mind that there is a difference between being upright and being truly balanced!

Caution your students to check that there are no other skiers coming from above before starting out across the slope.

1. Demonstrate how to traverse in a neutral position (described in the *Alpine Level II Study Guide*). Maintaining the hips over the feet, look at—and point the navel toward—the apex of the next turn. This aligns the upper body and hips toward the new turning direction. Allow the uphill ski and boot to travel about half a boot length ahead of the downhill ski and boot. The uphill foot, knee, hip, and shoulder therefore lead across the hill.

This is the same countered position you developed in short turns.

2. Have your students practice what you have just shown them. They should allow their skis to travel forward, with edges across the hill. The steeper the hill, the higher the edge angle will be. The goal is to traverse while maintaining balance so the skis track smoothly and consistently on an even path across the snow.

Students should feel most of their weight over the arch of the downhill foot and strong contact of the shin toward the inner side and the tongue of the downhill boot. They should also feel soft pressure on the uphill shin toward the uphill or outer side and against the tongue of the uphill boot.

3. Have the group practice traversing in the other direction.
4. To further develop stance and balance, have the students try traversing on only the downhill ski. Encourage the same stance and countered relationship of the upper body so that the inside (or uphill) half of the body is slightly ahead of the downhill half. Maintaining this relationship will help them stay balanced over the downhill ski. Have your group practice long enough for each member to succeed.

Note: Hand position is especially important. If the hands drop, or if the inside hand does not maintain its lead, the student will probably lose edge engagement, and ultimately lose balance.

Traversing on the Uphill Ski

When the group can traverse on the downhill ski, increase the challenge by having them traverse on the uphill ski. This traversing exercise is a bit more demanding. When done correctly, it anchors the movements and sensations of traversing with a countered upper body. The goal is to traverse on the uphill ski while it tracks forward without slipping sideways down the hill.

Demonstrate and have your students practice this progression for traversing on the uphill ski.

1. Balance on the uphill edge of the uphill ski. Point out that feeling strong contact of the uphill shin against the front cuff of the uphill boot promotes better balancing movements. Holding some muscular tension in the abdominal region and the lower back also helps maintain appropriate stance.
2. Hold the downhill foot off the snow so that it is slightly behind the uphill foot.
3. Try traversing while holding this position. It is important to keep the hips "open" (i.e., countered) and to maintain good upper body posture with quiet arms to balance over the outside edge of the uphill ski.

Hopping from Foot to Foot While Traversing

When students have achieved some success with traversing on the uphill ski, increase the challenge by having them hop from one foot to the other as they traverse. Hopping from foot to foot develops balance, edge control, and flexion and extension movements.

Have students practice this progression following your demonstration.

1. Traverse on both skis with a countered upper body position.
2. Lift the uphill foot while continuing to traverse.
3. Flex the downhill leg progressively, then extend in the knee and ankle quickly enough to push the hips up, with the ski leaving the snow.
4. Land on the uphill ski while you maintain the lead with the inside half of the body (a countered relationship).
5. Flex the uphill leg and make a quick, powerful extension to hop off of the snow.
6. Land again on the downhill ski.
7. Repeat this exercise in the opposite direction.

Note: Choose the terrain for this exercise with some caution. If the terrain is too steep, it may intimidate your students and make it difficult for them to succeed. The sooner they can succeed with a new activity, the more they will trust your direction. If your students find this exercise too difficult, you can add an intermediate step between steps two and three. After having your students traverse on one foot, have them step from ski to ski before hopping from ski to ski.

Traversing with Edge-set and Release

The movements for releasing the edges are just as important as those for engaging them. Edge control requires the ability to create the appropriate edge angle for the task at hand. Edge engagement and release actions depend on tipping movements of the legs and feet. To enhance your students' edge-control movements, have them practice both engaging and releasing edges while traversing.

1. Establish the proper posture and alignment for traversing. This includes tightening the abdominal muscles and slightly curving the spine. Relax tall so that all joints are slightly bent. Stand with your hips countered. It may be helpful to imagine that you are making a medium-radius turn; the hips and chest should face the apex of that imaginary turn. Feel most of your weight over the downhill arch, and therefore the downhill ski. Feel contact of the shin toward the uphill side of the tongue of the downhill boot. Feel soft pressure of the uphill shin toward the uphill side of the uphill boot tongue.
2. Aim the skis slightly off perpendicular across the fall line. The path that the skis take is the key for doing this exercise successfully. Aiming the skis down the fall line causes students to go so fast that they lose accuracy. This exercise is one of precision, so a slower speed is mandatory.
3. Traverse 10 to 15 feet forward and across the hill. The amount that the skis are tipped onto their corresponding edges depends on slope steepness. The goal is to traverse while maintaining balance so that the skis track smoothly and consistently on an even path across the snow.
4. Roll your ankles and knees into the hill, tipping the skis onto their corresponding edges. Your already slow speed will decrease as the skis quickly grip or bite in the snow. A small degree of pivoting may occur when you set your edges.
5. Reduce the edge angles (between the skis and the snow) by extending slightly so that the skis return to tracking along their original path. The track that the skis make on the snow measures the success of this task! The traversing tracks should be smooth cuts in the snow. The edge-set and release tracks indicate brief interruptions in a consistent, traversing path.

Adding a Sideslip to the Traverse

Build on the movements of the previous exercise by adding a sideslip in the middle of the traverse. This exercise further enhances the tipping movements of the legs and feet by exploring both sides of the edging spectrum.

1. Continue with the traverse and the edge-set movements previously described.

2. Once you have set your edges and have slowed to a stop, release the edges with a more deliberate straightening movement of the legs.

3. Roll or point the knees slightly downhill so the skis slip down a vertical path.

4. Allow the skis to slip 12 to 15 feet, then engage the edges by tipping the feet and knees uphill.

When accurately executed, the skis will begin to track across the hill, establishing a new traverse. Measure your student's success by examining the tracks their skis made in the snow. The track left by the traverse should be the same as described previously. The sideslipping track should follow a vertical path straight down the fall line.

Note: Set realistic goals. A Level 7 or 8 student may not achieve the degree of precision described, yet this degree of precision is imperative for a Level III candidate instructor. These exercises develop accurate, controlled edging movements. As students progress toward more dynamic medium-radius turns, they need the accuracy and subtle control movements they learn from these exercises.

Falling Leaf Sideslip

Build on the previous exercises by adding some active twisting (rotary) movements of the feet and legs. Teach this variation of the falling leaf exercise, which combines fore and aft balance, tipping (edging) movements and subtle

guidance (twisting movements). When well-executed, this exercise also develops upper and lower body separation. The objective is to slide forward and backward within a corridor in a criss-cross fashion.

1. Define an imaginary corridor or area for sideslipping which has a fairly decent pitch and is away from skier traffic. For more experienced students, teach this exercise on small bumps or rough terrain with hard snow conditions. The corridor should be approximately two to three ski lengths wide.

2. Adopt an athletic posture while standing predominantly on the outside ski. Keep your hips slightly countered, or open, toward the fall line. The uphill shoulder, knee, and foot will lead.

3. Without rocking or moving the body, press toward the tips of the skis while slipping forward. More pressure or weight toward the balls of the feet moves the skis forward. Gently twisting the feet and skis uphill will add to the exercise.

4. As friction builds (because the skis are edged and turning slightly uphill), the skis come to a stop.

5. Allow the pressure (or weight) to move toward the heels while you maintain the same amount of edge engagement. The skis then begin to slip diagonally backward.

6. Begin to twist the feet gently so that the tips of the skis drift downhill faster than the tails.

7. As the skis begin to slow again, press onto the balls of the feet to get the skis moving forward so you can repeat the exercise.

At this stage, students have a fairly broad range of experience relative to traversing and engaging and releasing edges. This range of experience helps them learn to engage the edge of the ski progressively as they make a more aggressive medium-radius turn.

Note: On some occasions, and with some students or groups, you may choose to use these exercises in the order in which they are presented. On other occasions, you may choose to use only one or two of these options, or you might choose to change the order in which you present the exercises. Your decisions should be based both on your experience and upon the outcome you and your students are seeking.

Skating

Once students have sufficiently developed their edging and steering movements, help them develop foot-to-foot movements. Skating is often introduced at the intermediate phase to help teach foot-to-foot movements for weight transfer and to help students learn to be more mobile on flat sections of terrain. Skating promotes the sensation of moving forward with the skis while the legs work both laterally and vertically.

Your upper body adopts a strong posture which is slightly curved due to active contraction of the abdominal muscles. Your legs work smoothly and efficiently underneath a quiet, stable upper body. You can use the following progression to teach students how to skate for the first time or to review the moves for students who have already been introduced to skating.

Teach this progression on an easy blue slope with little skier traffic.

1. Start at the side of the trail.
2. From a flexed position over the downhill ski, describe and statically demonstrate an extension that you direct forward and across the uphill ski. You execute this movement by pushing off of the original ski while propelling your body forward. In order to push off from the ski, it must be edged.
3. As your weight transfers to the new ski, begin to flex the ankle and knee while rolling the ski onto its edge. To remain centered, emphasize light pressure on the tongue of the boot.
4. Repeat the movements as you push back to the original ski.
5. Demonstrate the same movements while skiing toward your group. Tip your leg to edge the ski while flexing. Repeat the demonstration, this time going away from the group. Try to repeat the skating from foot to foot at least two or three times without stopping.
6. Give your students the opportunity to try skating, then have them practice.

When students have difficulty with this exercise, it is usually due to a lack of edge engagement, or from standing too tall and without sufficient flex in the ankle. Emphasize tipping the leg to edge the ski during ankle flexion.

Skating Across the Hill

Skating across the hill is an exercise that helps develop assertive movements during which the upper body continually moves slightly ahead of the feet.

Before starting, look uphill for oncoming skiers.

1. Align your body with a distant object across the slope.
2. Skate across the slope while targeting your body toward a distant landmark.

Emphasize the movements of the downhill foot and leg. For example, increase the tipping movements of the downhill ski to create a solid platform from which to skate.

Feel strong contact between the ball and arch area of the foot and toward the front and inside of the shin against the tongue of the boot.

Focus on moving forward from an extended downhill leg. Feeling the hamstring muscles stretch on the downhill leg and pressure on the ball of the foot are good indicators that the lower body, feet, and legs are propelling the hips and upper body forward.

Skate Turns

After you have taught your students to skate across a slope, teach them to skate into a turn. There are many variations of skate turns—so be creative.

1. Skate three times across the hill.
2. On the third skate, move onto the new (uphill) ski and twist that foot toward the fall line while rolling onto the inside edge so that you initiate a turn. Extend the uphill leg and commit all your weight to that ski as you tip the ski over onto its inside edge by rolling the foot and leg.

   Applying more weight over the ball and arch of the uphill foot while tipping it engages the sidecut of the ski. Extending the uphill leg moves the body across the skis, downhill, and toward the new turn as the ski tips enter the fall line.
3. Try to maintain balance and pressure over the inside edge as you continually tip and turn the ski back across the fall line.
4. After completing that turn, skate across the hill three times. Extend off of the uphill ski after the third skate.

1000 Steps

To further develop students' body position over the outside ski, commitment to the turn and an active movement of the body across the skis, introduce 1000 steps turns. This exercise is similar to skating across the hill and into the turn. In this exercise, however, ask students to skate continually from one foot to the other, both while moving across the hill and into the new turn. Have them create a platform on the outside ski, then push off onto the uphill ski so they can reposition the old ski. In essence, they should be seeking to gain some elevation while skating across the hill between turns.

1. Skate across the hill at a shallow angle away from your group. Show active flexion and extension in the process.
2. As you near the edge of the trail, skate onto the uphill ski.
3. Roll the uphill ski onto the inside edge and begin to skate into the next turn.
4. Continue the skating movements. To keep the skis turning, reposition each ski toward the intended turn each time you lift the ski off of the snow.

If your students have difficulty with any aspect of this exercise, break it down into its component parts. Also consider introducing or having your student practice the exercise on flatter terrain. Thousand steps is extremely valuable for developing and enhancing five of the six basic movement patterns of skiing:

• adjusting balance along the length of the skis;
• twisting the feet and legs to engage and release the edges;
• tipping the feet and legs to engage and release the edges;
• moving from foot to foot to transfer weight; and
• flexing and extending legs to control pressure.

As the students learn the 1000 steps exercise, they begin to develop hip angulation to edge their skis. This is especially true as they extend against the downhill ski to skate from the downhill foot.

Javelin Turns

To further develop the countered relationship, balance, and progressive edging, introduce javelin turns. Javelin turns enhance good posture, allowing efficient tipping movements. Traversing on the uphill ski is a lead-in drill for your students. Both exercises share common skill and movement patterns by developing hip counter and angulation.

Hip counter keeps the hips open and aligned toward the upcoming turn after exiting from the old turn. In other words, hip angulation helps the students stay in balance as the ski is continually tipped and turned through the arc.

Start on shallow terrain.

1. Begin by traversing while holding the uphill ski off the snow. While suspending the ski in the air, point its tip down the hill so that you are actually holding it above the downhill ski. This action opens up the hips so that they face more down the hill than across the hill.
2. Execute this traverse in both directions.
3. Then, start the traverse on the uphill ski. Begin to steer the ski down the hill and into a turn. At the same time, point the tip of the (new) lifted inside ski across the tip of the turning ski. Emphasize a countered stance and hip angulation.
4. Repeat this exercise in the opposite direction. If your students are having difficulty with the exercise, have them practice one turn at a time until they are comfortable with it.
5. Begin to link (medium-size) javelin turns. Once you have finished a turn, swing the inside ski parallel to the outside ski and transfer weight onto it. As you initiate the next turn, cross the tip of the new lifted inside ski over the outside ski. The goal is to maintain balance over the downhill ski throughout the turn.

Feel strong contact over the downhill arch and press the inside ankle bone into the side of the boot. Angle the upper body away from the hill, so that you feel a stretch along the side of the back (the latissimus dorsi muscle). Hold your hands in front of your body. You should angle your entire body so that it balances over the inside edge of the downhill ski. It is critical that you feel support underneath the downhill arch onto the big toe area and avoid the tendency to sit back.

Leapers

Leapers incorporate all the basic movement patterns of skiing and are appropriate for developing the mechanics of a medium-radius turn. Leapers are considered to be a variation of hop turns because they utilize a hop to get the skis off the snow, with the turn itself being initiated in the air.

Because leapers are initiated in the air, they are an appropriate choice for situations where either snow or terrain makes it difficult to initiate a turn.

To introduce this exercise, choose a run that is not intimidating for your group. A steep pitch is acceptable for very strong students, although a more moderate pitch benefits all levels of students.

1. Start by traversing across the slope.
2. While traversing, flex to prepare for the hop that initiates the new turn.
3. Hop vertically, using a pole plant for stability. While in the air, steer the skis slightly downhill and toward the new turn.
4. Absorb the impact of the landing by flexing the knees and ankles. During flexion, tip the skis onto their edges while continuing the guiding movements you began in the air.
5. Continue to increase the edge angle as the turn develops. This creates a solid platform from which to hop to initiate the next turn.
6. Give students an opportunity to practice this version of leapers.
7. Show them how to change edges in the air so that they land on the new set of edges rather than on flat skis. This requires the tipping movements of the feet and legs to take place in the air.
8. As the group improves in their ability to change edges in the air, have them reduce the hop and extension so that the skis

remain on the snow during the transition. With practice, this transition becomes quick and direct.

Uphill Christies

At this stage, students have all of the basic movements necessary to make strong, medium-radius turns. To make the turns truly dynamic, they need to learn what a ski can do when it is actively edged and pressured, plus how to continue to guide skis during the turn. Uphill christies are excellent for helping students learn these movement combinations. This exercise is also effective for developing shape at the bottom of the turn.

Choose an area that has low skier traffic. Have your students practice uphill christies after you demonstrate the exercise.

1. Face your body and skis about 45° from the fall line.
2. Begin to glide across the hill on that 45° line.
3. Press onto the ball of the downhill foot while feeling pressure on the front, inner part of the boot tongue. This movement engages the edge and cause the ski to bite into the hill. With patience, the ski will bend into an arc and turn uphill.
4. Have your students practice this exercise in both directions until they can engage the edge so that the ski creates an incomplete arc into the hill.
   If the tail of the ski washes out, the student is too far forward. If the ski tracks on its

edge and runs straight, the student is too far back on the heels.
5. Gradually have your students work the starting point closer and closer toward the fall line. Throughout this progression, encourage your students to actively move their legs while holding the upper body quiet. They should turn their skis under their upper body so that they finish in a countered relationship.
6. Demonstrate different degrees of inward movement during the uphill christie.

Explain that the further you move your hips in while flexing in the knees and ankles, the more the ski will turn. Also highlight the fact that the skis continue to arc, even though the turn shape gets tighter.

Applying the Uphill Christie Movements to Turns

When the students can start in the fall line and still make an accurate arc, using subtle guidance in conjunction with edge engagement, they will be ready to apply this movement to a series of turns.

1. Lead the group through a series of turns. First, unweight the skis with a vertical extension and steer them into the fall line. Once you reach the fall line, stop the active twisting movement that you used to initiate the turn and replace it with an uphill christie to make the second half of the turn.
   Finally, start the next turn by transferring your weight and

extending to release the edges and slightly unweight the skis so you can repeat the uphill christie.

2. Have your students practice this combination of movements until they are quite confident with them.

3. Have your students regulate the degree of flexion and inward movement during the second half of the turn to vary the turn shape of the uphill christie. Using the uphill christie to finish the second half of the turn creates a strong turn finish in which the ski itself creates much of the turn shape.

4. Explain to your students how this movement combination applies to different snow conditions. In general, the harder the snow, the more you can tip the skis up onto their edges. In softer snow, a little less tipping and more active guidance, controlling twisting of the feet and legs, is far more appropriate. If you encounter a combination of conditions, accept this as an opportunity to explore different skill combinations.

5. As your students become confident and proficient in using the uphill christie movement to create the second half of the turn, have them reduce the strong steering movements sooner in the turn. Instead of steering reasonably flat skis all the way to the fall line before the uphill christie, ask them to steer only long enough to initiate the new turn.

Almost as soon as their edges change and they steer their skis toward the new turn, your students should begin to flex their legs and ankles and tip them progressively inward. This flexion should last all the way through the arc in order to control edge angles and pressure over the skis throughout the turn.

It may be helpful to break the turn into imaginary thirds.

• During the first third of the turn, extend to unweight and steer the skis.
• During the second third of the turn, reduce the twisting effort and replace it with forward and inward tipping movements of the legs and feet.
• During the last third of the turn, begin to reduce the edge angles by progressively relaxing the muscles of the legs while transferring weight to the new ski.

At first, this approach may lead to a rather abrupt extension movement, but it allows students to develop a good sense for how and when to tip and pressure skis. Increasing the edge angles creates more pressure on the skis by reducing the surface area of the ski that is in contact with the snow. Flexing keeps the pressure from increasing too quickly and also allows students to continually guide the skis. With practice (and guidance), students learn to make the extension more progressive.

In spite of the fact that they are not putting as much effort into twisting the skis, there will still be some rotary motion. Due to contin-

uous inward tipping of the feet and legs, femoral rotation provides some (passive) rotary input to the skis. The more students tip their legs (during flexion), the more femoral rotations occurs. As edge angle increases, the skis continue to bend, creating a tighter arc.

By now, students will be making high-level, medium-radius turns. Lead them through a playful session of experimentation. Have them vary the inward movement to find out how tightly they can make the skis turn without losing balance. Have them ski sections at a variety of speeds. How far can they move inward at slower speeds? Your group will soon discover that slower speeds require them to combine more active twisting movements with tipping movements. Higher speeds will allow far more inward movement and require less active twisting movements.

Apply the same guided discovery teaching style to steeper and flatter terrain, and to various snow conditions.

The information in this section should provide you with plenty of possibilities for progressions. Be creative in how you construct your progressions to provide your students with many different results. Have fun with it!

Technical Aspects of Skill Development

Balancing Movements

Balance is the single most important skill in skiing because without it, students will never achieve the fine motor control necessary to advance in their skiing. The ability to maintain dynamic balance requires ongoing and continuous movements. Balancing movements consist of pushing the feet forward and pulling them back under the hips to maintain a centered stance within the balance zone.

This balance zone runs roughly from just in front of the toe piece of the binding to just behind the heel piece, and it is unrealistic to think that one can balance within a smaller zone, such as the arch of the foot.

In skiing, small adjustments can affect how the ski interacts with the snow. Standing too far forward will cause the tips of edged skis to bite and the tails to slip; standing too far back on the heels will cause the skis to "rail out" and run, leaving you out of balance (back and inside).

Balance is also affected by how you hold the upper body while skiing. Bending forward ("breaking") at the waist frequently puts a student too far forward on the skis. It can also be a compensating movement to try to get pressure toward the front of the ski for a student who stands with his or her ankles too straight. Countering movements and a countered relationship between the hips and upper body also aid in balance and help create a strong stance for advanced skiing.

In any given turn, the balance point on the skis changes from forward when beginning the turn to centered over the feet and skis throughout the bulk of the turn

itself. Many of the exercises in this chapter help develop the movements necessary to move the balance point over the skis fore and aft while skiing.

Lateral balance is also an important part of the big picture. The movements used to maintain lateral balance include foot-to-foot movements for weight transfer and turn initiation and an inward movement of the hips (center of mass) during the turn to create angulation.

Angulation, which includes the inclination or tipping of one part of the body against another part, results in an increased edge angle between the ski and snow to maintain balance while edging. For example, moving the hips in toward the center of the turn and the shoulders away from the center of the turn results in hip angulation.

Rotary Movements

In medium turns, rotary movements are a function of carefully controlled twisting movements of the feet and legs. Many of the exercises in this chapter require subtle control of the direction of the ski, and students achieve this control by a combination of tipping their feet and legs to engage the ski edges and "pointing" their feet in the desired direction.

They use a similar combination of tipping and twisting movements of their feet and legs to guide their skis. As students roll the foot toward the big toe side (inside edge) during the initiation of a turn (everting), the long bone of the shin (tibia) rotates inward. This

leads to a rotation of the thigh (femur) from the hip joint, which gives direction to the outside ski. They direct the inside ski by tipping the inside leg toward the center of the turn, which causes the femur of the inside leg to rotate externally, thereby guiding the inside ski through an arc similar to that of the outside ski.

In such exercises as skating, skate turns, and 1000 steps, students twist both legs and skis independently and actively, though subtly. In leapers, students turn both skis simultaneously to steer the skis in the air. They must execute this steering carefully to keep from over-turning the skis during the unweighted portion of the turn.

Javelin turns and uphill christies employ a combination of subtle twisting movements of the feet and legs and active edging movements to tip the skis onto their edges. The steering movements are primarily a by-product of the tipping movements which cause the bones of the leg and the hip joint to rotate.

Edge-control Movements

Edge-control movements begin with tipping the feet inside the ski boots. As the turn develops, edging movements involve the knees and ultimately, the hips. Through flexion during the second half of the turn, the skis are "skied" back under the body. As this happens, edge angles are reduced. The angulation is released or undone in the reverse order in which it was executed. If hip angulation was achieved, the hips become less involved as the skis begin to come back toward the body. As the hips become less involved, knee angulation becomes the dominant form of angulation until the skis are sufficiently underneath the upper body so that only feet and ankles are still tipped into the hill.

This sequence of events happens quickly, without giving you enough time to focus on any one form other than the main one (usually hip angulation in a medium turn). The edges are ultimately released in the transition from one turn to the next as the feet are tipped down the hill and toward the new turn.

The exercises in this chapter develop edging skills from the feet up, beginning with the traverse exercises and introduce or develop edging through hip angulation with 1000 steps and javelin turns.

Hip angulation causes the outside leg to be extended enough for the bones of the upper and lower leg to align. It is also necessary to counter with the hips and upper body when holding the outside hand over the outside ski. This counter is important for balance.

Countering with your upper body allows you to face your hips and chest more down the hill than toward your skis so that as you move your hips further inside (to increase edge angles), you can move the upper body more efficiently toward the outside ski to maintain better balance.

Edging movements of the inside leg are developed throughout this chapter but especially in the traverse exercises. Traversing on the uphill ski and hopping from foot to foot while traversing require active

and accurate edging movements of the inside leg. These exercises also help develop balance on the inside leg and foot.

Pressure-control Movements

You control pressure through the movements of extending and flexing the legs, by increasing or decreasing edge angles, or by moving from one foot to the other. The timing and/or combinations of these movements control whether pressure is increased, decreased, or maintained during a turn.

The movements you commonly use to execute a medium turn lead to a gradual increase in pressure from the moment you initiate the turn. As you tip the skis toward the intended turn, the increase in the edge angle reduces the amount of surface area of the ski that is in contact with the snow. The less the surface area, the greater the pressure. As the turn develops, pressure continues to build as the forces of the turn begin to align after the fall line. To control this increase and to keep the skis from becoming overloaded (and thus chattering), you flex progressively during the second half of the turn.

Generally speaking, you use an unweighting movement to lighten pressure prior to turn initiation. The most common form of unweighting in a medium turn is up-unweighting. As you begin to extend, pressure actually increases but not as much as it would otherwise because the skis are flattening at the same time (because you are rolling your feet toward the new turn). When the extension reaches

its highest point, the skis will become momentarily light, at which point you can easily redirect (steer) toward the next turn.

While we tend to think of flexion as reducing the pressure on the skis (because the mass of the body is moving toward the pull of gravity), flexion can also be used to increase pressure. In such exercises as skating and 1000 steps, pressure increases during flexion because the outside ski is actively tipped higher on its edge during flexion. In this example, pressure continues to increase as you extend against the edged ski. Pressure increases during flexion in uphill christies for the same reason.

The combinations of movements described above are only some of the possibilities available for creating, reducing, or controlling pressure. You are encouraged to continue exploring possible movement combinations with the ski school trainers at your resort.

Questions: Medium Turns

1. Fill in the blank:
    Dynamic balance means balancing while _____.

2. You move your legs and feet to maintain dynamic balance while moving down the hill.
    What are the three directions of movement?

    _____

    _____

    _____

3. Circle the best choice:
    The falling leaf exercise will develop (foot-to-foot movements for weight transfer) /
    (upper and lower body separation).

4. Fill in the blank:
    According to the study guide, when students have difficulty
    with the skating exercise, it is usually because they are: _____.

5. 1000 steps develops or enhances five of the six basic movement patterns of skiing.
    Name three of these movements:

    _____

    _____

    _____

6. Define angulation.

    _____

    _____

7. Circle the best choice:
    Knee angulation is (stronger) / (weaker) than hip angulation.

8. Choose the best answer:
    What type of pitch is appropriate for teaching leapers to all levels of students?
    A.   Shallow
    B.   Moderate
    C.   Steep

9. Fill in the blanks:

A) Sometimes the tail of the ski washes out during an uphill christie. This is caused by the weight being:

_____

B) Sometimes, the ski ends up tracking on its edge and running straight during an uphill christie. This is caused by the weight being:

_____

10. Circle the best choice.

In general, the harder the snow, the (less) / (more) you tip the skis up onto their edges.

11. Choose one or more of the following:

Medium-radius turns offer the following advantages over short-radius turns:
A. They are less fatiguing so they might be a better alternative for skiing at the end of the day when your legs are tired.
B. They give you more time to experience and feel different movements as you execute them.
C. They are better for exploring the movements necessary to develop a carved turn.

12. True or false:

When making turns, there is actually no such thing as a balanced position.

13. Circle the best choice:

For medium-radius turns, you should ("stand tall") / (stand with your spine slightly curved).

14. Choose the best answer:

In a traverse, you should:
A. Face in the direction of travel
B. Look toward the apex of an imaginary turn
C. "Bow to the valley"

15. True or false:

Having the uphill hip lead during a traverse is an example of countering.

16. The study guide describes a number of exercises involving traversing. Name two of these.

_____

_____

17. The study guide describes two possible results of dropping a hand or not continuing to lead with the uphill hand while traversing. Name one of these.

_____

_____

18.   True or false:
        Relaxing your stomach muscles and the muscles of your lower back will help you maintain an appropriate stance for traversing on the uphill ski.

19.   Choose one or more of the following:
        Hopping from foot to foot while traversing will help develop:
        A.   Balance
        B.   Edge control
        C.   Flexion and extension movements
        D.   Steering

20.   If you find that your students are having trouble learning to hop from foot to foot while traversing, the study guide suggests adding an intermediate step. What is this?

        _____

21.   Choose the best answer:
        At what angle should you have your students begin their traverse in the traverse with an edge-set and release exercise?
        A.   Perpendicular to the fall line
        B.   45° from the fall line
        C.   Not quite perpendicular to the fall line

22.   True or false:
        In the traverse with an edge-set and release exercise, you first traverse a few meters across the hill and then roll your ankles and knees into the hill. It is crucial to avoid any pivoting when you set your edges.

23.   True or false:
        In the traverse with a sideslip exercise, the sideslip should follow a vertical path straight down the fall line.

24.   Choose one or more of the following:
        Exercises which combine fore and aft balance, tipping movements, and twisting movements are:
        A.   Traversing on the uphill ski
        B.   Traversing with an edge-set and release
        C.   Hopping from foot to foot while traversing
        D.   Traversing with a sideslip
        E.   Falling leaf sideslip

25.   On what type of terrain does the study guide suggest teaching more experienced students the falling leaf sideslip exercise?

        _____

26. Choose the best answer:
About how wide should the imaginary corridor for the falling leaf sideslip exercise be?
A.   A ski length
B.   Two to three ski lengths
C.   Five to seven ski lengths

27. True or false:
In the falling leaf sideslip exercise, after pressing toward the tips of the skis while slipping forward, gently twist the feet and skis uphill.

28. Circle the best choice:
When skating across the hill, increase the tipping movements of the (uphill) / (downhill) foot and leg.

29. Choose the best answer:
In the skate turns exercise, you first skate across the hill. You twist the uphill foot toward the fall line while rolling the ski onto its inside edge so that you initiate a turn. At what point do you commit your weight to the turning ski?
A.   Prior to tipping the ski onto its inside edge
B.   As you tip it over onto its inside edge
C.   After initiating the turn

30. True or false:
In an uphill christie, when the turn shape gets tighter, the skis lose their ability to arc.

31. Choose the best answer:
In 1000 steps, while skating across the hill between turns you should try to:
A.   Gain some elevation
B.   Stay at the same elevation
C.   Lose some elevation

32. What exercise does the study guide recommend as being a good lead-in drill for the javelin turns exercise?

_____

33. True or false:
In javelin turns, it is critical to feel support from the downhill arch and the heel.

34. True or false:
The leapers exercise incorporates all of the basic movement patterns of skiing.

35. Circle the best choice:
The further (in) / (out) you move your hips while flexing in the knees and ankles, the more the ski will turn.

36. Circle the best choice:
You should tip your skis onto their edges more during an uphill christie on (softer snow) / (harder snow).

37. Circle the best choice:

   Increasing the edge angles during a turn will reduce the surface area of the ski that is in contact with the snow, therefore (increasing) / (reducing) the pressure on the skis.

38. Circle the best choice:

   (Extending) / (Flexing) will keep the pressure that builds during a turn from increasing too quickly.

39. Choose one or more of the following:

   Breaking at the waist:

   A.   Frequently puts a student too far forward

   B.   Can be a compensating movement for students who stand with their ankles too straight

   C.   Results in an increased edge angle between the ski and the snow

40. True or false:

   Countering movements and a countered relationship between the hips and upper body help your stance and balance.

41. Circle the best choice:

   Throughout the bulk of any given turn, the skier should be (centered over the feet and skis) / (forward).

42. Choose one or more of the following:

   Which movement(s) help(s) maintain lateral balance?

   A.   An inward movement of the hips

   B.   Foot-to-foot movements

   C.   Pushing the feet forward and pulling them back

43. Circle the best choice:

   Moving the (hips) / (shoulders) toward the center of the turn and the (hips) / (shoulders) away from the center of the turn results in hip angulation.

44. Fill in the blank:

   As you roll the foot toward the big toe side during the initiation of a turn (eversion), the tibia rotates inward. This leads to a rotation of the _____ , which gives direction to the outside ski.

45. Choose one or more of the following:

   Which exercise(s) involve(s) independent leg action?

   A.   Leapers

   B.   1000 steps

   C.   Skating

   D.   Skate turns

46. Circle the best choice:

   In javelin turns and uphill christies, (the steering movements are primarily a by-product of the tipping movements) / (the tipping movements are primarily a by-product of the steering movements).

47. Choose the best answer:

When making a medium-radius turn, you first angulate in your ankles, then in your knees, then in your hips. Later in that turn, you first release or undo the angulation in your:

A. Ankles
B. Knees
C. Hips

48. Choose the best answer:

The main form of angulation in a medium turn is often:

A. Ankle angulation
B. Knee angulation
C. Hip angulation

49. Choose one or more of the following:

Which exercise(s) develop(s) edging primarily through hip angulation?

A. Javelin turns
B. Traversing
C. Traversing with an edge-set and release
D. Traversing on the uphill ski
E. Hopping from foot to foot while traversing
F. 1000 step turns

50. Circle the best choice:

Countering with your upper body allows you to face your hips and chest more down the hill than toward your skis so that as you move your hips further (inside) / (outside) to increase edge angles, you can move the upper body more efficiently toward the (inside) / (outside) ski to maintain better balance.

51. Name two exercises described in the study guide which help develop balance on the inside leg and foot.

_____

52. Choose one or more of the following:

To control pressure:

A. Decrease edge angles
B. Increase edge angles
C. Move from foot to foot
D. Lengthen your legs
E. Shorten your legs

53. At what point in a medium radius turn do your skis become lightest?

_____

54. Fill in the blank with one or more words:

To control the increase in pressure and to keep your skis from becoming overloaded (and thus chattering) during the second half of the turn you should _____ .

55. Choose one or more of the following:
     When you exit the fall line during a medium turn, pressure normally:
     A.   Increases
     B.   Does not change
     C.   Decreases

56. Choose one or more of the following:
     During which exercise(s) does pressure actually increase during flexion?
     A.   Leapers
     B.   1000 steps
     C.   Skating
     D.   Uphill christies

Answers: Medium Turns

1. *In motion or moving.* Dynamic balance is balance in motion.

2. *Up and down, fore and aft, and side to side.* To maintain dynamic balance while moving down the hill, you move your legs and feet up and down, fore and aft, and side to side underneath the upper body.

3. *Upper and lower body separation.* When well executed, the falling leaf exercise will develop upper and lower body separation.

4. *Not engaging their edges enough or are standing too tall without sufficient flex in the ankle.* When students have difficulty skating, it is usually due to a lack of edge engagement, or from standing too tall without sufficient flex in the ankle.

5. 1000 steps is valuable for enhancing and/or developing five of the six basic movement patterns of skiing:
    *   Adjusting balance along the length of the skis
    *   Twisting the feet and legs to engage and release the edges
    *   Tipping the feet and legs to engage and release the edges
    *   Moving from foot to foot to transfer weight
    *   Flexing and extending legs to control pressure

6. *Angulation* is the creation of an angle within the body that results in an increase of the edge angle of the ski in the snow to maintain balance while edging.

7. *Weaker.* Knee angulation is not as strong as hip angulation. Hip angulation is often used in medium and long-radius turns because it allows the bones of the outside leg to be stacked on one another. This makes hip angulation stronger than knee angulation.

8. B. A steep pitch is acceptable for teaching leapers to very strong students, although a *more moderate* pitch will benefit all levels of students.

9. A) *Too far forward.* B) *Too far back.* While practicing uphill christies, if the tail of the ski washes out, the student is too far forward. If the ski tracks on its edge and runs straight, the student is too far back on the heel.

10. *More.* In general, the harder the snow, the more you can tip the skis up onto their edges.

11. A, B, & C. Medium-radius turns are less fatiguing so they might be a better alternative for skiing at the end of the day when your legs are tired. The slower cadence of a medium turn allows you more time to experience and feel the different movements as you execute them. Medium-radius turns are also better for exploring the movements necessary to develop a carved turn.

12. *True.* When making turns, there is actually no such thing as a balanced position.

13. *Stand with your spine slightly curved.* For medium radius turns, you should stand with your spine slightly curved and keep your joints bent slightly.

14. B. In a traverse you should *look toward the apex of an imaginary turn.*

15. *True.* Having the uphill hip lead during a traverse is an example of countering.

16. *Traversing, traversing on the uphill ski, hopping from foot to foot while traversing, traversing with an edge-set and release, and adding a sideslip to the traverse* are the exercises in the study guide that involve traversing.

17. *Loss of edge engagement and ultimately loss of balance.* If the hands drop during a traverse, or if the inside hand does not maintain its lead, the student will probably lose edge engagement and, ultimately, balance.

18. *False.* The exact opposite is true. Instead of relaxing your stomach muscles and the muscles of your lower back, you want to hold some muscular tension in the abdominal region and the lower back to help maintain the appropriate stance for traversing on the uphill ski.

19. A, B, & C. Hopping from foot to foot while traversing will help develop balance, edge control, and flexion and extension movements.

20. *Have them step from ski to ski before they hop from ski to ski.* If your students are having trouble learning to hop from foot to foot while traversing, you can add an intermediate step. After having your students traverse on one foot, have them step from ski to ski before they hop from ski to ski.

21. C. In the traverse with an edge-set and release exercise, students should aim their skis *slightly off the perpendicular route across the fall line.* Aiming the skis too close to the fall line will cause them to go so fast that they will lose accuracy. The path that the skis take is the key for doing this exercise successfully. This exercise is one of precision, so a slow speed is mandatory.

22. *False.* In the traverse with an edge-set and release exercise, a small degree of pivoting may occur when you set your edges after traversing a few meters forward and across the hill.

23. *True.* In the traverse with a sideslip exercise, the sideslip should follow a vertical path straight down the fall line.

24. E. The falling leaf sideslip exercise builds on the traversing exercises by adding some active twisting (rotary) movements of the feet and legs. The falling leaf exercise described in the study guide combines fore and aft balance, tipping (edging) movements, and subtle guidance (twisting movements). When well executed, this exercise will also develop upper and lower body separation.

25. *Small bumps or rough terrain.* For more experienced students, the study guide suggests teaching the falling leaf sideslip exercise on small bumps or rough terrain with hard snow conditions.

26. B. The imaginary corridor for the falling leaf sideslip exercise should be two to three ski lengths wide.

27. *True.* Step 3 of the falling leaf sideslip exercise consists of the following: Without rocking or moving the body, press toward the tips of the skis while slipping forward. Feeling more pressure or weight toward the balls of the feet moves the skis forward. Gently twisting the feet and skis uphill will add to the exercise.

28. *Downhill.* When skating across the hill, emphasize the movements of the downhill foot and leg. For example, increase the tipping movements of the downhill ski to create a solid platform from which to skate.

29. B. On the third skate of the skate turns exercise, move onto the new (uphill) ski and twist that foot toward the fall line while rolling onto the inside edge so that you initiate a turn. Extend the uphill leg and commit all your weight to that ski *as you tip the ski over onto its inside edge* by rolling the foot and leg.

30. *False.* In an uphill christie, the further you move your hips in while flexing in the knees and ankles, the more the ski will turn. The skis will continue to arc, even though the turn shape gets tighter.

31. A. In 1000 steps, while skating across the hill between turns you should try to *gain* some elevation.

32. *Traversing on the uphill ski.* Traversing on the uphill ski is a good lead-in drill for the javelin turns exercise. Both exercises share common skill and movement patterns by developing hip countering and angulation movements.

33. *False.* In javelin turns, it is critical to feel support from underneath the downhill arch to the big toe area since it is easy to sit back in this exercise.

34. *True.* Leapers incorporate all of the fundamental movements of skiing and are appropriate for developing the mechanics of a medium-radius turn.

35. *In.* The further in you move your hips while flexing in the knees and ankles, the more the ski will turn.

36. *Harder snow.* In general, the harder the snow, the more you can tip the skis up onto their edges. In the softer snow, a little less tipping and more active guidance (controlled twisting of the feet and legs) is far more appropriate.

37. *Increasing.* Increasing the edge angles during a turn will create *more* pressure on the skis by reducing the surface area of the ski that is in contact with the snow.

38. *Flexing.* Flexing will keep the pressure that builds during a turn from increasing too quickly and will also allow you to continually guide the skis.

39. A & B. Bending forward (breaking) at the waist frequently puts a student *too far forward* on the skis. It can also be a compensating movement to try to get pressure toward the front of the ski for a student who stands with his or her ankles too straight.

40. *True.* Countering movements and a countered relationship between the hips and upper body also aid in balance and help create a strong stance for advanced skiing.

41. *Centered over the feet and skis.* In any given turn, the balance point on the skis changes from forward when beginning the turn to centered over the feet and skis throughout the bulk of the turn itself.

42. A & B. The movements used to maintain lateral balance include foot-to-foot movements for weight transfer and turn initiation and an *inward movement* of the hips (center of mass) during the turn to create angulation.

43. *Hips, shoulders.* Moving the hips in toward the center of the turn and the shoulders away from the center of the turn results in hip angulation.

44. *Femur or thigh.* As you roll the foot toward the big toe side (inside edge) during the initiation of a turn (everting), the long bone of the shin (tibia) rotates inward. This leads to a rotation of the thigh (femur) from the hip joint, which gives direction to the outside ski.

45. B, C, & D. In such exercises as *skating, skate turns and 1000 steps*, students twist both legs and skis independently and actively, though subtly. In leapers, students turn both skis simultaneously to steer the skis in the air.

46. *The steering movements are primarily a by-product of the tipping movements.* Javelin turns and uphill christies employ a combination of subtle twisting movements of the feet and legs and active edging movements to tip the skis onto their edges. The steering movements are primarily a by-product of the tipping movements which cause the bones of the leg and the hip joint to rotate.

47. C. In a medium-radius turn, you release or undo the angulation in the reverse order in which you executed it. Since you originally angulated in your ankles, then in your knees, and finally in your hips; later in that turn you would begin to release the angulation in your hips first. As the hips become less involved, knee angulation becomes the dominant form of angulation until the skis come back under the body enough so that only feet and ankles are still tipped into the hill.

48. C. The main form of angulation in a medium turn is often hip angulation.

49. A & F. The exercises in this chapter introduce or develop edging through hip angulation with *1000 steps and javelin turns*. The traverse exercises develop edging skills from the feet up.

50. *Inside, outside.* Countering with your upper body allows you to face your hips and chest more down the hill than toward your skis so that as you move your hips further inside (to increase edge angles), you can move the upper body more efficiently toward the outside ski to maintain better balance.

51. *Traversing on the uphill ski and hopping from foot to foot while traversing.* Traversing on the uphill ski and hopping from foot to foot while traversing require active and accurate edging movements of the inside leg. These exercises also help develop balance on the inside leg and foot.

52. A, B, C, D, & E. You control pressure through the movements of extending and flexing the legs, by increasing or decreasing edge angles, or by moving from one foot to the other. The timing and/or combinations of these movements control whether pressure is increased, decreased, or maintained during a turn.

53. *At the end or highest point of the extension.* In a medium radius turn, the skis will become momentarily light when the extension reaches its highest point.

54. *Flex progressively.* In order to control the increase in pressure and to keep your skis from becoming overloaded (and thus chattering) during the second half of the turn, you flex progressively.

55.   A. The movements you commonly use to execute a medium turn lead to a gradual increase in pressure from the moment you initiate the turn. As you tip the skis toward the intended turn, the increase in the edge angle reduces the amount of surface area of the ski that is in contact with the snow. The less the surface area, the greater the pressure. As the turn develops, pressure continues to build as the forces of the turn begin to align after the fall line.

56.   B, C, & D. In such exercises as *skating and 1000 steps*, pressure increases during flexion because the outside ski is actively tipped higher on its edge during flexion. In this example, pressure continues to increase as you extend against the edged ski. Pressure increases during flexion in the *uphill christie* exercise for the same reason.

Notes

Moguls

Lesson Outcome

Students learn to link turns in small moguls on moderate to steep terrain. As their skills improve, they learn tactical approaches to moguls, a wider variety of movement patterns, and how to vary turn shapes and sizes.

Mogul skiing may be the first and for some, the only off-piste situation or ungroomed snow condition that students experience. Most resorts do not groom the entire mountain on a daily basis. As students continue to develop and challenge themselves, they encounter moguls more frequently. Such variations in the skiing surface are a reality of skiing, and you have both the opportunity and responsibility to teach students to deal with them successfully.

Several considerations need to be addressed when introducing students to mogul skiing for the first time. Ideally, students who have taken lessons on a consistent basis and were exposed to moguls during Level 5 and 6 lessons. Even so, many students tend to avoid bumps because they find them too challenging.

Good bump skiing demands not only good balance and a solid stance, but the ability to adjust that stance quickly and repeatedly. This means that balancing movements need to be refined to the point where they become automatic. You need to give your students lots of guidance and practice to help them

Photo 4. Turning in Moguls

develop fore, aft, and lateral movements of the feet, ankles, and knees, which allows them to remain upright as the terrain changes.

Initially, the most important element of mogul skiing is the ability to turn the feet quickly. Students gain a high degree of confidence, even in their first mogul runs, from knowing that they can twist their feet quickly and powerfully to make the skis turn.

Mogul skiing is depicted in photo 4.

Review Edging and Pivoting Movements

Demonstrate and start the exercise on a stretch of groomed snow that is steep enough to sideslip easily.

1. Stand with your skis across the fall line, and with your body facing down the fall line. Flex the ankles and knees. Hold your hands just above waist level—comfortably in front of your body with your elbows about as

far forward as the front of your chest.
2. Release your edges to sideslip by gradually extending your legs. Extend by moving your knees and ankles downhill over your skis. Allow your skis to drift laterally downhill while maintaining a horizontal orientation (keeping the skis across the fall line).
3. Re-engage the edges by flexing slightly and rolling the feet, ankles, and knees back into the hill.

Have your students practice this movement in both directions until they can release their edges, allow their skis to slip sideways for a few feet, and then re-engage their edges without losing fore-aft or lateral balance. Be careful to reinforce the flexion and extension movements associated with releasing and engaging the edges.

For your students to successfully ski moguls, they will need to be able to quickly change the direction their skis are pointing. To help them develop this, have them add some active pivoting movements to the sideslipping they have been practicing. For this part of the learning segment, it is important for them to keep their feet and legs aligned directly under their upper bodies. Develop their ability to quickly change the direction the ski tips are pointing by having them extend to release the edges, and quickly twist their feet and legs to pivot the skis.

From a static position (with edges engaged and the upper body facing downhill), demonstrate and have your students practice extending and releasing their ski edges. Have them plant the downhill pole to help stabilize the upper body in an anticipated (countered) position. (Anticipation refers to the relationship between parts of the body in which the upper and lower parts of the body are somewhat twisted against each other.) This twisting results in a stretching of the trunk muscles, which, when the edges are released or when the skis are unweighted, helps the body realign. Anticipation is a means of enhancing turn initiation.

Linked Hockey Slides or Pivot Slips

Linking pivots and sideslips into linked hockey slides or pivot slips (see Short Turns for a description of pivot slips) teaches students to control the direction their skis face and to quickly redirect their feet

and skis. Both are essential skills for skiing moguls.

Choose a section of the hill to use as a practice area. Visually define the parameters of a corridor for your group. If the snow is well groomed, lines left in the snow by the grooming equipment may be used to define your corridor. (The lines will be roughly 25 feet apart.) If you cannot find lines left by grooming equipment to define your corridor, you may want to use the trees along one edge of the run to define one side of the corridor. You can designate the other side by dividing the run into imaginary thirds, or by drawing a line in the snow by setting an edge with one ski and wedging with the other for a few yards down the hill. Use any creative means you choose.

Once you have defined a corridor, have your students practice linking the hockey slides or pivot slips inside the parameters. In order to maintain a good fall line orientation, students need to remain centered over their skis. If their balance point varies along the length of their skis, the skis tend to wander back and forth across the hill rather than following a more direct fall-line path. Don't insist on strict maintenance of the corridor. Rather, focus on pivoting the skis, maintaining the upper body down the hill, and coordinating pole use while allowing the skis to continue slipping down the hill.

Remember—balance is a range of movements, rather than a position! Consider balance to be a zone that goes from just in front of the toe piece of the binding to just behind the heel piece. As the skis

start up the front or top of a bump, they will slow down and the student's balance will move toward the front of the zone; as the skis travel down the back of the mogul (and therefore accelerate), the student's balance will tend to move toward the back of the zone. To help stay centered, students may have to push their feet slightly forward as they slow down, then pull them back under the hips again so that pressure returns to the middle of the foot. In photo 5, the skier demonstrates fore/aft balance in moguls.

Photo 5. Fore/Aft Balance in Moguls

Falling Leaf

Before taking your group to the moguls, develop their ability to control balance along the length of their skis with the falling leaf exercise. This exercise describes a pattern on the snow that resembles the swaying motion of a leaf as it falls to the ground the skier zig-zags down the slope. The exercise helps students gain the feeling of how to balance by pushing the feet forward and pulling them back. These balancing movements also control pressure along the length of the ski.

1. Statically, with your feet across the hill, demonstrate how to adjust fore/aft balance by pushing your feet forward and then pulling them back under your hips.
2. Explain and then demonstrate how dynamically pointing the skis slightly downhill, then pulling them back under the hips, causes the ski tips to engage and climb into the hill.
3. Before your skis come to a stop, demonstrate how to push your feet forward, which adds pressure to the tails of your skis. This changes your balance point in relation to the skis, and the tips of the skis pivot on the snow without you having to make an active pivoting movement.

   As your forward momentum stops (due to the friction of the skis drifting across the snow after they have pivoted uphill), you begin to glide backward across the slope. As your skis slide backward, the pressure on the tails causes the skis to climb uphill, just as they did when they were traveling forward. This is true as long as you maintain pressure on your heels.
4. Pulling your feet back under your body (to again put pressure on the balls of the feet) changes the balance point over the skis and causes the skis to pivot and slip across the snow. As the backward motion stops, the ski tips point downhill and the skis begin to glide forward.

5. Have your students practice this exercise enough times to get a good feel for changing the pressure and balance along the length of the foot.

Add Edging and Steering

After you have had your students make a few passes sliding forward and backward across the hill, have them add tipping (edging) and twisting (steering) movements of the feet and legs by incorporating a 180° pivot, roughly in the middle of the forward glide across the hill. Demonstrate and then have your students try this exercise.

1. Repeat the forward glide of the falling leaf exercise.
2. When you reach the middle of the trail, roll your feet, ankles, and knees aggressively into the hill while twisting your feet and legs powerfully uphill.
3. Once you have pointed your feet straight uphill and have pushed them forward (just as in the falling leaf), roll your feet from the uphill to the downhill side to flatten your skis.

4. Twist your feet so that your ski tips point back toward the downhill side. This exercise will help your students begin to understand how much they can control their skis with their feet. It will also facilitate their ability to control the skis as they begin to ski the moguls.

Where to Turn in the Moguls

The group now has the basic skills to begin skiing in the moguls. Take them to an area of the mountain that has small bumps, or at least to a place where the bumps are somewhat spread out. Either of these situations will be appropriate for the next step (applying pivot slips in moguls).

Before turning your group loose in the bumps for the first time, it is a good idea to briefly describe where to ski in the bumps. For many people, trying to see a route through a mogul field is like trying to read a newspaper in an unknown foreign language. Start by discussing terminology. The terminology for mogul skiing is shown in figure 1.

Fig. 1. Mogul Terminology

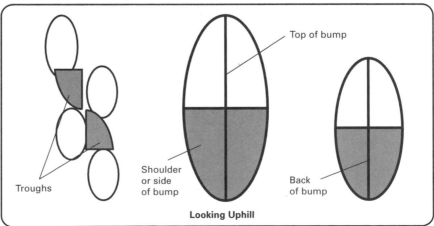

Troughs
Shoulder or side of bump
Top of bump
Back of bump
Looking Uphill

The most common terms include:

- the top (crest) of the bump—the highest part of the mogul;
- crestline—high portion that runs the entire vertical length of moguls (starting a turn on the top of a bump could mean starting it anywhere along that vertical line);
- shoulder (side) of the bump—the steep, banked area on either side of the top;
- back of the bump—the downhill half below the top (sometimes steeper than the pitch of the run it sits on!); and
- troughs—ruts that form between the end of one bump and the beginning of the next (especially pronounced when soft snow that exists soon after a snowfall or in the warm part of a springtime day gets compacted quickly or freezes).

Some students will want you to show them where to start a turn in the bumps. It is easiest for them to pivot their skis on the top of each bump. The path a skier might take in pivot slips is shown in figure 2. Once they have started the turn (pivot slip), they can sideslip down the back side of the mogul while still controlling speed and maintaining balance. It may be helpful to quickly draw a few bumps in the snow so that you can show your students where to ski.

Pivot Slips in the Moguls

1. Demonstrate two or three pivot slips, starting each one on the top of a bump. If possible, try to demonstrate toward the group. Executing the pivot slips without

Fig. 2. Skier's Path for Pivot Slips

Looking Uphill

an edge-set between pivots allows a more continuous flow down the hill. If students are tentative, suggest that they use an edge-set to create a stronger sense of control.

Be sure to show active flexion and extension movements (to release the edges), and a pole plant on the top of each bump to help stabilize the upper body and promote balance.

2. Initially, have each of your students try two or three pivot slips. If your group is somewhat timid, have them ski only one pivot slip at a time, at first.

3. Once the students can link two or three pivot slips, have them gradually link more. Encourage them to use the pushing and pulling movements of their feet to stay in balance as terrain changes in their first few turns in the moguls.

4. Once they become confident in their ability to link more pivot slips, increase the length of the practice segments, and give the group the chance to choose their own lines through the bumps. At first, it may be easier for your students to remain in a static, flexed position over their skis rather than use both flexion and extension. Staying in a relatively low stance does little to control the pressure on the skis, but helps the students remain balanced because their hips will be closer to the snow (i.e., lower center of gravity). Starting each pivot slip on the top of a bump makes the skis easy to turn because there is so little resistance. When the ski is on top of a bump, only the center of the ski contacts the snow. As the tips and tails are free, there is very little resistance to pivoting the skis, and redirecting them is quite easy.

5. When your group can successfully link pivot slips in the bumps, encourage them to begin using a more active range of flexion and extension. Also, have them practice some pivot slips that incorporate an edge-set before each turn to give them another means of controlling speed (other than by creating friction through sideslipping). Continue to anchor these movements when you introduce the idea of "absorbing" moguls. Absorption refers to flexing and extending the legs as the skier moves over uneven terrain, while the upper body remains more quiet.

Photo 6. Blocking Pole Plant

Developing Pole Use in the Moguls

The students' accurate use of poles may have suffered during the previous segment of the lesson. Good pole use is invaluable in mogul skiing because it helps stabilize the upper body. As the skis approach a mogul, they tend to slow down because they are suddenly going uphill. This may pitch the body forward. In order to block slowing the momentum of the upper body, students should plant the pole on top of the mogul as the skis begin to climb it. They can also use the pole plant as a signal to trigger the next turn. A blocking pole plant is depicted in photo 6.

As discussed in the Short Turns chapter, the pole helps anchor the body in an anticipated relationship. When the torso is somewhat twisted, the legs realign themselves with the torso when the edges are released. Adding an active pivoting movement of the feet and legs to this unwinding effect provides quick, powerful turn initiation.

Reaching down the hill to plant a pole can help to start a new turn from a position this is out of balance. If students find themselves sitting back when they are ready to start a new turn, the pole plant provides a point of balance plus a point of deflection to start the turn it provides a support to help recover balance. The pole is only be of value if the student has already swung it forward. This enables students to plant the pole when they need it the most. Work with your students to help them understand proper timing of the pole plant.

1. Ski across the hill toward a mogul. While showing good hand position, swing the downhill pole forward. Good arm and hand position in shown in photo 7.
2. As your ski tips begin to ride up the side of the bump, plant the pole tip on the crest of the bump.
3. Pivot your skis on the top of the bump and let them drift down the back of the same bump.
4. Swing the other pole point forward and plant it on the crest of the next bump as your skis begin to ride up onto the bump. It may helpful to ask your students to reach for the top of the next bump with the tip of the ski pole. Have each of your

Photo 7. Arm and Hand Position in Mogul Skiing

students try the same movement, then practice it enough to be comfortable with the timing. It is important to anchor pole usage well before moving on to new information and movements.

Introducing and Applying Absorption

The next step toward advancing mogul skiing skills is to introduce the idea of absorption.

Traversing in a mogul field is an easy way to practice absorption.

1. On a trail that is not overly crowded, traverse from the edge of the run toward the first mogul.
2. Demonstrate absorption by skiing over one or two moguls.
3. Ask students to use their legs somewhat like the suspension system in a car. When the tire hits a bump in the road, the shock absorber allows the wheel to move toward the car. Once the wheel has traveled past the bump, the spring pushes the wheel back to the road. This keeps the wheels in contact with the road, even on irregular surfaces.

    The legs should work in the same way. As the ski tip encounters a mogul, students should let their muscles soften enough to allow the feet to travel toward the hips. On the crest of the bump, where they pivot their feet, their legs are at their shortest. As their skis begin to slide down the back side of the bump, their legs should be

lengthened again. Not only does this keep the skis on the snow, it also leaves them in a position to absorb the next mogul.

4. Ask your students to try this exercise one at a time.
5. As they succeed, have them lengthen the distance of the traverse and increase the number of moguls they ski.

Adding Absorption to Linked Pivot Turns

Now your students are ready to add the new element of absorption to linked pivot turns in the bumps. Have them continue to initiate turns on the tops of the bumps while using the relatively passive flexion and extension of the legs that absorption requires.

If the group seems hesitant or is having difficulty grasping or executing absorption, give them more time to practice absorbing without having to turn.

1. Demonstrate how to traverse across three moguls, absorbing each as you go, and then pivot the skis on top of the third bump to make a new turn.
2. Repeat this in the opposite direction.
3. Have your students try what you have just shown them.
4. After the students have made a couple of traverses and pivoted turns in each direction, have them turn on top of the second mogul.
5. Finally, when they seem comfortable with this, have them begin to turn on top of each bump while absorbing.

It does not take long for your students to realize how absorption smooths out the terrain. At this stage, the students have the skills to successfully link smooth turns through a mogul field. Because they will more than likely be having a good time, give them a number of practice runs to enjoy their new-found skills.

Developing Advanced Mogul Skills

So far, any discussions of line, or where to ski in the bumps, have been confined to simply telling the students to start the turn on the top of the bump. To continue making gains in the bumps, students must understand the available line options.

The easiest line to see and therefore to follow is over the tops of bumps—that is why it was used in the introductory mogul lesson. Skiing that line, however, requires the student to go over some very irregular terrain. Absorbing the terrain will help, but large variation between high and low spots can disrupt balance, especially at higher speeds. If the bumps are fairly well spread out, suggest that your students ski around the moguls as much as possible. This causes fewer disruptions to balance and challenges both their visual skills and their discipline. (However, since it is not possible to ski around every bit of rough terrain, absorption is still a necessary movement.) Skiing around the bumps allows students to make turns that are longer and rounder (less pivoted).

Skiing around the Moguls

Show your students how to ski around moguls.

1. Ask your students to look down the hill for high and low spots. (No doubt they will be able to identify the high spots!)

   Suggest that they time their turns to avoid, as much as possible, skiing over the tops of the bumps, and instead ski around them. Remind them that this rounder turn requires pivoting less and guiding their skis more constantly throughout the turn.

2. Demonstrate a few turns skiing a version of the line you want them to take.

3. Invite the group to spread out and try skiing a similar line for themselves. As their skills improve, or if the bumps are not particularly well-spaced, you can teach another option using a much shorter turn shape. In this option, the students will ski from one trough to the next, but with a round turn.

A typical mogul field is shown in figure 3. The shaded areas represent the troughs, or ruts, between the bumps. The troughs are the low spots. The figure represents the intended line through the tight bumps and deeper troughs.

Skiing the Troughs with a Rounder Turn

Skiing this line still requires you to pivot your skis, but you also need to tip them much more actively

Fig. 3. Line Through a Mogul Field

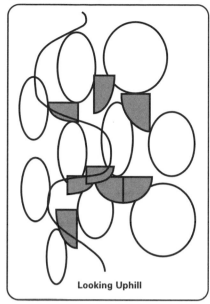

Looking Uphill

toward the new turn during the transition from one turn to the next.

1. Start by identifying the trough of a mogul for your group.

   Explain where to place the skis to begin the turn. Rather than lining the skis up directly with the trough (which would gain speed with each turn), tell your students to point the skis more across the hill and slightly across the edge of the trough. The trough creates a high spot of its own lower than the moguls above and below it, but higher than the rest of the snow between the bumps. This high spot provides a good place to begin the next turn. Also, explain that skiing across the trough still requires you to use some absorption, leaving their legs bent at the end of the turn.

2. Demonstrate a line that travels across the trough at the finish of one turn, and then banks off the shoulder of the bump that is just to the side of the bump you are

turning around. Guide the skis through the bottom of the turn and across the next trough.

3. While still flexed, roll your feet, ankles, and knees down the hill toward the new turn, while aggressively twisting the skis toward the new turn. The same movements that serve to release the edges will, when continued, re-engage the skis on the opposite set of edges. When there is little resistance to turning, as on the top of a bump, the tipping movement serves to steer the skis.

4. Extend while continuing to direct the skis by twisting your feet and legs.

5. As the skis come through the bottom third of the turn, begin to relax the muscular tension to absorb the terrain. This combination of movements puts the skis onto the new set of edges and provides some degree of pivoting. The pivoting, however, occurs on edged skis instead of flat skis. The edge engagement helps shape the new turn, and results in an arced, short turn rather than a skidded one.

Hop Turns in the Moguls

In order for your students to succeed in skiing this aggressive and athletic line, they need quickness. Hop turns on groomed terrain are a good way to help develop both the mechanics and agility necessary to ski bumps well. Not every student will want to ski this line, but is an exciting challenge for some. Assure students that they can ski bumps with any number of lines, so the choice is theirs.

You can also use hop turns as an exercise in the bumps, provided that there are a few bumps with tops that are a couple of ski lengths long.

1. Start at the top of the long mogul with your skis across the hill and edges engaged.
2. Plant your pole on the crest of the bump and flex your knees and ankles.
3. Extend explosively and twist your feet while in the air so that you land on the crest of the same mogul with the opposing set of edges.
4. Try to execute three or four hop turns on the top of the same bump.
5. Have the group members try the same task, but ask them to make only a couple of hop turns.

Take this exercise in small doses because it is demanding and can be very fatiguing.

As your students continue to improve and begin to ski faster in the moguls, their contact with the bumps may seem jarring. Absorption alone may not be enough to keep their skis on the snow. If this is the case, suggest that they try a more active form of absorption. Pulling the feet toward the hips just before contacting the bump can reduce the impact. This retraction becomes absorption as the bump pushes the students' feet toward their hips. The timing takes practice, so if you introduce retraction in the bumps, be patient and provide encouragement.

The information presented here represents quite a bit of teaching ammunition. However, there are other lines and options available for mogul skiing. If you run out of tactics or ideas, consult your ski school trainer.

Questions: Moguls

1. Choose one or more of the following:
    Anticipation:
    A. Is a relationship in which the upper and lower parts of the body are twisted against each other
    B. Is when the upper and lower parts of the body uncoil in opposite directions
    C. Stretches the trunk muscles
    D. Can make initiating turns easier

2. Adding an edge-set after the sideslip in the pivot slip exercise will cause the skis to stop abruptly.
    What does the study guide suggest having your students do to stabilize their upper body?

    _____

3. Choose one or more of the following:
    Use the following exercise(s) to teach students how to control the direction their skis face and
    how to quickly redirect their feet and skis:
    A. Sideslip
    B. Traverse
    C. Linked hockey slides
    D. Pivot slips

4. Choose the best answer:
    About how wide a corridor does the study guide suggest for linked hockey slides or pivot slips?
    A. One ski length
    B. Six feet
    C. Twenty-five feet

5. Choose one or more of the following:
    When students first learn linked hockey slides or linked pivot slips, they should focus on:
    A. Facing the upper body down the hill
    B. Keeping the skis sliding directly down the fall line
    C. Pivoting the skis
    D. Using the poles
    E. Staying within the corridor

6. Choose the best answer:
    The balance zone for linked hockey slides or pivot slips:
    A. Goes from just in front of the toe piece of the binding to just behind the heel piece
    B. Goes from half way between the tip and the toe piece to half way between the heel piece and the tail
    C. Goes from the tip to the tail of the ski
    D. Is under the arch of the foot

7. Circle the best choice:
    As your skis travel down the back of a mogul, your balance will tend to move toward the
    (back) / (front) of the balance zone and your skis will (accelerate) / (slow down).

8. Choose one or more of the following:
    You can adjust your fore-aft balance by:
    A.   Flexing and extending
    B.   Pulling and pushing your feet
    C.   Tipping your legs into the hill

9. Circle the best choice:
    To help you stay centered as your skis travel up the front of the bump and then down the back, you may
    have to (push your feet slightly forward and then pull them back) / (pull your feet back and then push
    them forward).

10. Choose the best answer:
    In the falling leaf exercise, pointing the skis slightly down the hill, then pulling them
    back under the hips will cause:
    A.   The tails to engage
    B.   The tips to engage
    C.   The skis' edges to engage from tip to tail

11. Circle the best choice in each of the following three paragraphs:
    In the falling leaf exercise, after pulling your feet back under your hips, pushing your feet forward will add
    pressure to the (tails) / (tips) of your skis.

    This will change your balance point in relation to the skis, and the (tails) / (tips) of the skis will pivot on the
    snow without your having to make an active pivoting movement.

    As your forward momentum stops, you will begin to glide backward across the slope. As your skis slide
    backward, the pressure on the tails will cause the skis to climb uphill, just as they did when they were
    traveling forward. This will be true as long as you maintain pressure on the (balls of your feet) /
    (heels of your feet).

12. Write the number of the correct definition from the right hand column for each of the terms in the left-hand
    column in the space provided:

    Mogul Terminology

Term	#	Definition
A. Top	_____	1. The steep banked area on either side of the top.
B. Shoulder	_____	2. The downhill half below the top, which is sometimes steeper than the pitch of the run the bump was formed on.
C. Trough	_____	3. The highest part of the mogul itself. Often a crest line that runs the entire vertical length of a mogul.
D. Back	_____	4. A rut that forms between the end of one bump and the beginning of the next. It is especially pronounced when the soft snow that exists soon after a snowfall (or in the warm part of the day during the springtime) gets compacted quickly or freezes.

13. On which part of the mogul is it easiest to pivot the skis?

    _____

14. Fill in the blank with one or more words:
    For tentative students, the study guide suggests adding _____ between pivots in the moguls.

15. Choose one or more of the following:
    Staying in a relatively low stance without using flexion or extension movements when first executing pivot slips in the moguls will help your students:
    A.   Control the pressure on their skis
    B.   Remain balanced
    C.   Neither of the above

16. Fill in the blank:
    Adding an edge-set before each turn in the pivot slips in the moguls exercise will help control _____.

17. Choose one or more of the following:
    Deflection in the moguls:
    A.   Causes the weight to transfer to the heels
    B.   Involves using a pole plant to redirect the body
    C.   Can help get a new turn started

18. Circle the best choice:
    When practicing absorption while traversing the bumps, your legs will be at their shortest on the (back) / (front) of the bump.

19. True or false:
    To teach your beginning mogul students a relatively passive form of absorption, have them pull their feet toward their hips just before they contact the bump.

20. Choose the best answer:
    The easiest line to see and therefore to follow is:
    A.   Over the tops of bumps
    B.   Around the bumps
    C.   From one trough to another

21. Circle the best choice:
    Skiing (around the bumps) / (over the tops of the bumps) will cause fewer disruptions to balance.

22. Circle the best choice:
    A rounder turn around the moguls requires you to pivot (less) / (more) and to guide your skis more constantly throughout the turn.

23. Circle the best choice:
     When teaching your students to ski the troughs, you (should) / (should not) have them line
     their skis up directly with the trough.

24. True or false:
     The tipping movement you use to turn your skis on the top of a bump steers also the skis.

25. Briefly describe the more active form of absorption which the study guide suggests using in the moguls.

     _____

Answers: Moguls

1. A, C, & D. *Anticipation* is a term used to describe a *relationship between parts of the body in which the upper and lower parts of the body are somewhat twisted against each other*. This twisting results in a *stretching of the trunk muscles*, which, when the edges are released or when the skis are unweighted, will help the body realign. It is considered a means of *enhancing turn initiation*.

2. *Plant the pole.* To help your students improve their sense of control in the pivot slip exercise, have them add an edge-set after they have sideslipped. While setting their edges, they should make a solid pole plant to stabilize the upper body because the edge-set will cause their skis to stop abruptly.

3. C & D. *Linked hockey slides or pivot slips* teach students how to control the direction their skis face and how to quickly redirect their feet and skis. Both are essential skills for skiing moguls.

4. C. The corridor for linked hockey slides or pivot slips should be roughly *twenty-five feet* apart.

5. A, C, & D. In linked hockey slides or pivot slips, if your students' balance point varies along the length of their skis, the skis will tend to wander back and forth across the hill rather than follow a more direct fall-line path. At this stage, staying in the fall line is not important. You should have your students focus on *pivoting the skis, maintaining the upper body down the hill, and coordinating pole use* while allowing the skis to continue to slip down the hill.

6. A. The balance zone for linked hockey slides or pivot slips goes from *just in front of the toe piece of the binding to just behind the heel piece*. It is unrealistic to think that you can balance within a smaller zone, such as the arch of the foot.

7. Back, accelerate. As the skis start up the *front* or top of a bump, they will slow down and your balance will move toward the front of the zone; as the skis travel down the *back* of the mogul (and therefore accelerate), your balance will tend to move toward the back of the zone.

8. B. You can adjust your fore/aft balance by *pulling and pushing* your feet.

9. *Push your feet slightly forward and then pull them back.* To help stay centered while skiing moguls, you may have to push your feet slightly forward as you slow down while traveling up the front of a mogul, and then pull them back under your hips again so that pressure returns to the middle of the foot.

10. B. *The tips to engage.* In the falling leaf exercise, pointing the skis slightly down the hill, then pulling them back under the hips will cause the tips to engage and climb into the hill while the skis glide forward.

11. *Tails, tips, heels of your feet.* After pulling your feet back under your hips, pushing your feet forward will add pressure to the *tails* of your skis. This will change your balance point in relation to the skis, and the *tips* of the skis will pivot on the snow without you having to make an active pivoting movement. As your forward momentum stops (due to the friction of the skis drifting across the snow after they have pivoted uphill), you will begin to glide backward across the slope. As your skis slide backward, the pressure on the tails will cause the skis to climb uphill, just as they did when they were traveling forward. This will be true as long as you maintain pressure on the *heels of your feet*.

12. A = 3, B = 1, C = 4, D = 2.
    Mogul terminology:
    - The *top* of the bump is the highest part of the mogul itself. Often, especially in long bumps, the top is a crest line that runs the entire vertical length of a mogul. Therefore, starting a turn on the top of a bump could mean starting it anywhere along that vertical line.

    - The *shoulder* or side of the bump is the steep banked area on either side of the top.

    - *Troughs* are the ruts that form between the end of one bump and the beginning of the next. The troughs of moguls are especially pronounced when the soft snow that exists soon after a snowfall, or in the warm part of a springtime day, gets compacted quickly or freezes.

    - The *back* of the bump is the downhill half below the top, and is sometimes steeper than the pitch of the run the bump was formed on.

13. *On the top*. When you first teach pivot slips in the moguls, having your students start each pivot slip on the top of a bump will make the skis easy to turn because there is so little resistance. When the ski is on top of a bump, only the center of the ski is in contact with the snow. Since the tips and tails are free, there will be very little resistance to pivoting the skis and redirecting them will be quite easy.

14. *An edge-set*. Executing pivot slips in the moguls without an edge-set between pivots will allow a more continuous flow down the hill. If students are tentative, suggest that they use an edge-set to create a stronger sense of control.

15. B. At first, when executing pivot slips in the moguls, it may be easier for your students to remain in a static, flexed position over their skis than to use flexion and extension movements. Staying in a relatively low stance will do little to control the pressure on the skis, but will help your students *remain balanced* because their hips will be closer to the snow.

16. *Speed*. Having your group practice some pivot slips that incorporate an edge-set before each turn will give them another means of controlling their speed (other than by creating friction through sideslipping).

17. B & C. If students find themselves on their heels when they need to start a new turn, they can use a pole plant to provide a point of balance to *help redirect the body*. In this case, they "deflect" themselves around the pole to get *a new turn started*. This deflection can be an effective recovery tool.

18. *Front or crest*. When practicing absorption while traversing the bumps, their legs will be at their shortest on the crest (front) of the bump where they pivot their feet. Their legs will be lengthened again as their skis begin to slide down the back side of the bump. This will not only keep the skis on the snow, but will also leave them in a position to absorb the next mogul.

19. *False*. Pulling your feet toward your hips is a more active movement. You often teach students to actively pull their feet and legs back toward the body (by contraction of the hip flexors) for powder or crud.

20. A. The easiest line to see and therefore to follow is over the *tops of bumps*—that is why it was used in the introductory mogul lesson.

21. *Around the bumps.* Skiing *around the bumps* will allow students to make turns that are a little longer in size and rounder in shape (less pivoted).

22. *Less.* When having your students ski around the moguls, remind them that this rounder turn will require them to pivot *less* and guide their skis more constantly throughout the turn.

23. *Should not.* When teaching your students to ski the troughs, having them line their skis up directly with the trough would cause them to continue to gain speed with each turn. Instead, tell your students to point their skis across the hill more and slightly across the edge of the rut. The trough creates a high spot of its own lower than the moguls above and below it, but higher than the rest of the snow between the bumps. This high spot provides a good place to begin the next turn.

24. *True.* When there is little resistance to turning as on the top of a bump the tipping movements serve to steer the skis.

25. *Retraction or pulling the feet toward the hips just before the bump.* If absorption is not enough to keep your students' skis on the snow, suggest that they try a more active form of absorption. By actually pulling the feet toward the hips just before the feet contact the bump, they can reduce the impact. This retraction becomes absorption as the bump pushes their feet toward their hips.

Notes

Steeps

Lesson Outcome

Students learn to negotiate steep terrain with pivoting, edge-sets, and a blocking pole plant. Through exercises and practice, they learn to become more assertive and deliberate in their movements.

Skiing steep terrain is exciting and rewarding for advanced students. It provides the opportunity to explore new, often less crowded terrain. Although many instructors may be working toward a turn which is accurately guided with an appropriate blend of rotary, edging, and pressure-control skills, students who are venturing onto steep terrain for the first time will no doubt suffer some setbacks in turn accuracy. Help build confidence and re-establish their skill base. First, have your students focus on active rotary skills through pivoting their feet and skis to assure that they will be able to get their skis across the fall line quickly. This gives them the ability to control speed. After that, you can begin to work on application of skills. As in all upper level skiing, a balanced, centered stance is paramount to success. Other essential skills for entry-level skiing of the steeps include:

- quick, powerful steering movements;
- the ability to exert strong pressure against the outside ski to help support the platform of the skis;
- a strong pole plant to block and stabilize the upper body; and
- strong unweighting movements.

Before you introduce students to steep terrain for the first time, they need to be able to make short turns on moderate terrain with a solid pole plant. If they have not yet acquired these movements, spend some time developing short turns according to the progressions outlined in this study guide.

When introducing steep terrain, it is best to start on a somewhat moderate pitch.

Pivot Slips

Review the mechanics necessary for short turns by demonstrating and then having your students practice a series of pivot slips.

1. Begin with your skis across the fall line.
2. Demonstrate a vertical sideslip.
   - Face your upper body as directly downhill as possible, and hold your hands in front of your body so that you can swing your pole by moving your wrist.
   - Release your edges by tipping or rolling your feet, ankles, and knees down the hill.
   - Gradually extend in the ankles and knees to release the edges. It will be easier for your students to see the extension if you demonstrate it as viewed from the side.
3. As your skis begin to drift directly sideways, begin to flex your ankles and knees again while slowly tipping your ankles and feet back into the hill.
4. Have each of your students make the same movements; then repeat them in the opposite direction.
5. Demonstrate another sideslip, this time changing direction with an active twisting motion.
   Extend and tip your feet and ankles down the hill. At the same time, twist your feet and legs to steer your skis into the fall line. Continue the same twisting movement until the skis are pointed across the hill in the opposite direction, trying to keep the skis flat enough to continue sideslipping.
6. Begin to flex progressively while continuing to target the upper body downhill.
7. Extend again and twist the feet in the opposite direction, without coming a stop.
   Leaving the skis flat allows you to focus on twisting the feet and skis.
8. Have your students try the same movements.
9. As your students become proficient in twisting their feet and skis in both directions, while maintaining a vertical sideslip, have them add a pole swing and touch. The pole helps stabilize the upper body for turn initiation and edge change. They should plant the pole during the bottom of the flexion for this exercise.
   Have students practice swinging the pole while they are flexing their legs are so that the tip is forward and ready to be planted when they are at the lowest point in the flexion.

Hop Turns

If you have a group that is more athletic or aggressive, you can easily substitute hop turns for pivot slips. A hop turn is shown in photo 8. Hop turns encompass all of the skills necessary for skiing steeps, including:

- upper and lower body separation and independence;
- solid pole plant to stabilize the upper body;
- flexion and extension movements to unweight the skis;
- active twisting movements of the feet and legs to redirect the skis; and
- tipping the feet and legs to edge the skis when they return to the snow (to create a solid platform from which to hop again).

After demonstrating hop turns and having your students practice them, take the same exercise to a slightly steeper pitch. Add an edge-set at the bottom of the flexion of each turn to momentarily stop the forward (downhill) movement, then extend and steer in the opposite direction. The edge-set is valuable on steep terrain because it provides both a platform from which to move and a sense of control.

Moving to Steeper Terrain

At this point, the group should be ready for even steeper terrain. If possible, start the next set of exercises on a short pitch to reduce anxiety. You can gradually move to longer, steep pitches as the lesson

Photo 8. Hop Turn

A

B

C

progresses. The next set of exercises uses the skills you have just taught.

1. Demonstrate a forward and diagonal sideslip while maintaining upper and lower body separation. The friction of the edges scraping across the snow reduces speed.
2. After drifting forward and laterally for a few feet, set the edges by rolling the ankles and knees into the hill.
3. Plant the downhill pole at the same time to stabilize your body. This is necessary not only for balance, but to block your body. Because your body is moving forward at the same rate as your skis, once you set your edges the body continues to move downhill unless you block it with a solid pole plant.

   It may be necessary to focus on pole use in addition to the edge-set so that your students have their poles ready when they set their edges. When focusing on pole usage, use only the diagonal sideslip and edge-set. Have your students swing the pole forward while progressively flexing in a diagonal sideslip. Then have them drop the pole tip into the snow when they set the edges.
4. Have students practice these movements. At first, encourage them to engage their edges progressively to allow them time to adjust their balance as their skis slow down.

   As they make that adjustment, have them increase the intensity of the edging movement by engaging the edges more quickly.

5. When students are able to accurately time the edge-set and pole plant, show them how to initiate the next turn.

6. Extend quickly and twist your feet and legs powerfully to pivot the skis (just as in the pivot slips) back across the hill in the opposite direction.

7. Begin to flex progressively as you allow the skis to slip diagonally forward.

8. Repeat the edge-set and pole plant.

   Note that setting the edges on the top of a small bump may aid in the pivoting phase of turn initiation.

9. Once students have practiced enough to become comfortable with the movements and have gained confidence in their ability to negotiate the steep hill, have them begin to reduce the distance the skis drift laterally. They should flex a little more quickly and set their skis edges sooner. They should continue to use a pivoted initiation, but should try to link the turns a little more directly. Allow plenty of practice time to help anchor the movements as well as build confidence.

10. Have the group replace the diagonal sideslip after the pivot with a vertical one. If they need to, allow them to sideslip a few feet between edge-sets to recover their balance or to build confidence for the next pivot. They quickly realize that they can link pivoted turns in the fall line without having to slip very far between turns.

A common error at this stage is leaning into the hill. This happens instinctively as people move away from things that frighten them. Students who are apprehensive about the pitch of the hill may tend to drop the inside hand and shoulder at the end of a turn. If this happens, coach them to tip their shoulders toward the downhill ski. It may also be helpful to ask them to hold their uphill hand in front of their body. This not only helps keep them more balanced over the downhill ski, it also helps put them into a strongly countered or anticipated position.

Improving Short Turns in Steep Terrain

There is no substitute for practice time and mileage in skiing. This is especially true when learning to ski in upper level terrain and snow conditions. Guard against teaching too much too quickly. While your students may seem to continue to improve while they are skiing with you, it is the rare student who can assimilate all of what you may want to teach in a single lesson. Most students will forget what you have taught them unless you pace your lesson to provide considerably more practice time than you may think is necessary.

Only when your group appears to have assimilated the material outlined above should you begin to move beyond it. If you have the same students for a multi-day lesson, be sure to thoroughly review what you covered the previous day before moving on. Remember, these students are recreational athletes who are most likely on vacation! They enjoy the practice time.

To improve your students' skiing performance in steep terrain, you must create a more balanced application of skills. So far, you have taught them to pivot their skis to bring them back across the hill. This is an important element, because it gives them the ability to control their speed. Another more advanced means of controlling speed on steep terrain is to use a round, finished turn shape, rather than pivoting and edge-sets. Students will still have to use the same degree of pivoting in short turns, however, because even the most aggressively-shaped skis are incapable of making a pure carved turn with a radius small enough to control speed on steep terrain. This is certainly true for students who are still somewhat inexperienced on steep terrain.

To help your students make rounder, short-radius turns on steep terrain, teach them to engage the edges of their skis much earlier in the turning process. For now, the goal is to pivot the skis on their edges, as opposed to keeping them flat. The mere fact that the edges are engaged contributes to a slightly rounder turn shape because the sidecut of the skis will begin to interact with the snow. The added resistance of the edges will help students learn to use more progressive steering or guiding movements that last throughout the turn, rather than simply using a pivoting movement to start the turn.

To teach this more progressive guidance for steep terrain, try the following, once again on moderate to slightly steep terrain.

1. Have your students make pivot slips in a vertical corridor. Pay special attention to the timing of the pole swing and touch.

   Students should adopt a lower, more compact stance when moving from one pivot to the next. In other words, they should use less vertical motion to initiate change of direction.

   If they are having difficulty maintaining the corridor, it could be a stance problem. If necessary, spend a little time to be sure that their hips are over their feet and that they can maintain pressure on the balls and arches of their feet.

2. With the group gathered around you, demonstrate statically how to tip the skis onto their edges by rolling your feet, ankles, and knees into the hill.

3. Ask your group to make the same movements and watch them individually to make sure they are performing the movements correctly.

4. Explain that as they pivot their skis toward the next turn, they should roll their feet and ankles toward the turn as well. It may make sense to them to ask them roll their feet and ankles before they begin to pivot their skis. (In reality, the movements happen together because the act of tipping the feet into the new turn leads to a rotation of the thigh. Rotating the thighs gives some direction to the skis.)

5. Starting in a straight run in a low stance, demonstrate how to tip

your feet and ankles toward the intended turn while aggressively twisting your feet and legs.

6. Plant your pole and repeat the same movements in the opposite direction.

   A well-timed pole swing and plant will enhance your students' ability to execute the described movements. If the pole swing is slow, the student will not really be well-balanced and prepared to start the next turn. Encourage students to get ready for the next turn by beginning to swing their poles as soon as they have twisted their feet toward the next turn. This helps assure that they are ready for the next turn.

7. Have your students try these movements.

8. Show the group how to link a series of these turns in a narrow corridor. This results in turns that pivot on the edges, rather than on flat ski.

9. Have your students execute the same sequence of exercises.

   Emphasize the activity of tipping the feet, ankles, and finally the knees into the top of the new turn. Some students may make a less pivoted, longer-shaped turn. Explain the need for the active twisting of the feet and legs: since they will be heading back to steep terrain next, they still need to use plenty of steering to get the skis back across the hill for speed control. Keep in mind that it takes more time to pivot on the edges than on a flat ski. An active, rounder, and slightly longer turn shape is the goal.

Take the group back to steeper terrain and let them experiment with this new blend of skills. You will probably need to remind them to stay a little lower and tip the skis up on edge as they begin to pivot. With practice, they will end up making much rounder turns in the fall line.

Extension and Absorption

To continue improving your students' steep-skiing skills, teach them how to extend their legs after they have initiated the turn.

1. Extend the legs quickly, progressively, and continuously to apply pressure to the ski from the beginning of the turn. Extension should be directing the skis toward the fall line.

2. As you continue to actively twist your feet and skis through bottom of the turn, flex your legs gradually enough to make the movement last until you have guided your skis back across the fall line.

3. Without beginning to extend, tip the skis down the hill and start to pivot on the edges again. This movement pattern is essentially an extension-absorption pattern.

   The flexion in the second half of the turn allows the skis to continue through a clean, though quick, arc. Flexing correctly will allow the pressure that builds up on the skis after the fall line to be absorbed. Without such flexion, the ski becomes overloaded either bouncing and chattering in the snow, or loading so quickly that the resulting rebound causes students to lose their balance (with hips falling behind their feet). Such a mistake almost certainly leads to a loss of control. Flexion also allows the student to increase the edge angles during the second half of the turn, which means that the skis continue to bend and help shape the bottom of the turn.

This movement pattern is a little different from the extension-retraction pattern that you might teach for skiing in powder or crud. In powder or crud, you often have students actively pull their feet and legs back toward the body (by contracting the hip flexors). For steeps, the flexion is more passive, allowing the pressure of the snow against the bottom of the skis to help push the legs into a more flexed position. By yielding to the pressure, the student absorbs the pressure.

Progressive and lateral extension allows students to keep their skis in contact with the snow throughout the turn even on very steep terrain. As the students begin a new turn, the ground will seem to drop away. By staying lower during the transition and edge change, students can use the extension to "reach" their feet and skis toward the snow, thereby maintaining ski-snow contact throughout the turn.

These elements allow the hips and torso (the center of mass) to continue uninterrupted movement from one turn to the next. By tipping the feet, ankles, and knees

down the hill while the legs are flexed (changing the edges), the body is no long held inside the arc of the old turn. The result is that the body flows from one turn to the next.

This flow is enhanced by an active, well-timed pole swing which helps draw the upper body across the skis and down the hill, all in balance. Teaching students to move the hips across the skis before the edges have been released often leads to a disjointed, poorly-balanced turn entry.

Leapers

Try leapers to help your students work on correctly combining hip movement with active edge release. Your students should be able to link pivoted turns on their edges before you introduce leapers.

Use this progression on the steeps only with your highest-level groups.

1. On moderate to slightly steep terrain, demonstrate a series of three or four leapers. Initiate the turns with a vertical extension aggressive enough to leap the skis a few inches off the ground. This extension must come from the knees and ankles with the hips over the feet.

   Given the steeper terrain, a shorter version of a medium turn is probably the best radius for this exercise.

2. Steer the skis toward the fall line while in the air, and use the ankles and knees to soften or absorb the landing. Continue to steer the skis throughout the

rest of the turn.

3. Have the group try a few leapers. Pay attention to how much they steer the skis in the air (over-steering will result in landing with too high an edge angle and a loss of balance).

4. Once they can successfully leap, initiate the steering in the air and guide the rest of the turn on the snow, have them repeat the exercise, this time with the goal of landing on the new set of edges. To accomplish this, they must direct the leap both forward and across the skis.

5. Have them practice until they can land on the new set of edges and guide the rest of the turn on an edged ski.

6. On somewhat steeper terrain, have them repeat the leapers, again changing edges in the air. In order to accomplish the task, the students have to begin to change edges as they leap, which allows the hips to move across the skis without interruption.

7. As they succeed, have them eliminate the leap and replace it with tipping the feet, ankles, and knees toward the new turn. Gradually have them work the radius back into a short turn.

Remember that improvements on challenging, upper-level steep terrain may take a long time. Be patient and enthusiastic celebrate even the smallest achievements your students make along the way. These subtle victories help enhance your students' skiing experience and will prove tremendously rewarding for you!

Questions: Steeps

1. Name two of the essential entry-level skills for skiing the steeps given in the study guide.

    _____

    _____

2. Circle the best choice:
    In the pivot slip exercise, have your students begin to swing the pole forward while (flexing) / (extending) and have them plant their pole (at the bottom of the flexion) / (at the top of the extension).

3. What exercise does the study guide suggest substituting for pivot slips for a more athletic and/or aggressive class?

    _____

4. Circle the best choice:
    Before you introduce students to steep terrain for the first time, first make sure that they have the ability to make (medium-radius) / (short-radius) turns.

5. Choose one or more of the following:
    On steep terrain, the edge-set in a hop turn:
    A.   Helps control your speed
    B.   Provides a platform from which to move
    C.   Stabilizes the upper body

6. True or false:
    Having your students set their edges on the top of a small bump can aid in the pivoting phase of turn initiation.

7. Which exercise does the study guide suggest using to review the mechanics necessary for short turns?

    _____

8. In which direction(s) does the study guide recommend demonstrating the extension for pivot slips?
    A.   Fore and aft
    B.   Lateral
    C.   Vertical

9. What is one of the advantages mentioned in the study guide for having your students add an edge-set at the bottom of the flexion in hop turns?

    _____

10. Fill in the blank with the name of a physical property:
    A forward and diagonal sideslip reduces speed because of:

    _____

11. Why does the study guide recommend having your students add a solid pole plant to their edge-set (after sideslipping)?

    _____

12. Choose the best answer:
    If you focus on pole use in addition to the edge-set (in the exercise described above), you should use:
    A.   A diagonal sideslip
    B.   A vertical sideslip
    C.   Either a diagonal or a vertical sideslip
    D.   None of the above

13. True or false:
    Pivoting the skis to bring them back across the hill is a more advanced means of controlling speed than using a round, finished turn shape.

14. Choose the best answer:
    Which type of turn should you teach your students to help them control their speed on steep terrain?
    A.   Extension-retraction turns
    B.   Rounder short-radius turns
    C.   Shorter-radius carved turns

15. When linking pivot slips in a corridor, it may make sense to your students to think about rolling their feet and ankles before they begin to pivot their skis. In what order do these movements actually take place? (Rolling first, pivoting first, or simultaneously)

    _____

16. The study guide describes an exercise where you first extend the legs in the lateral plane until the skis reach the fall line and then flex your legs during the second half of the turn.
    A.   How does flexing correctly affect the pressure on the skis?

    _____

    B.   What can happen to your skis if you do not flex?

    _____

    C.   What effect does flexing have upon potential edge angles?

    _____

17. Choose one or more of the following:
    Often, having your students move their hips across their skis before they have released their edges
    A.   Improves the flow from turn to turn
    B.   Leads to a disjointed turn entry
    C.   Leads to a smoother turn entry

18. What size (radius) turn does the study guide suggest for the leapers progression?

    _____

19. Circle the best choice:
    If students have difficulty staying within the corridor in the pivot slips exercise, there could be a stance problem. If necessary, spend a little time to be sure that their (feet are out from under their hips) / (hips are over their feet).

Answers: Steeps

1. The essential entry-level skills for skiing the steeps given in the study guide are:
    *   active twisting movements of the feet and legs to redirect the skis;
    *   quick, powerful steering movements;
    *   the ability to quickly tip the skis onto their edges to create a solid platform;
    *   a strong pole plant to block and stabilize the upper body;
    *   strong unweighting movements;
    *   a balanced, centered stance; and
    *   upper and lower body separation and independence.

2. *Flexing, at the bottom of the flexion.* In the pivot slip exercise have your students practice swinging the pole while they are *flexing* their legs so that the point is forward and ready to be planted when they are at the lowest point in the flexion. Since they will need the pole to help stabilize their upper body when they initiate the turn and change edges, they should plant their pole during the *bottom of the flexion* for this exercise.

3. *Hop turns.* If you have a group that is more athletic and/or aggressive, you can easily substitute hop turns for pivot slips.

4. *Short turns.* Before you introduce students to steep terrain for the first time, first make sure that they have the ability to make short turns on moderate terrain with a solid pole plant.

5. A & B. The edge-set at the bottom of the flexion of each hop turn momentarily stops the forward (downhill) movement. It is helpful on steep terrain because it provides both a platform from which to move and a sense of control.

6. *True.* Having your students set their edges on the top of a small bump can aid in the pivoting phase of turn initiation.

7. *Pivot slips.* Review the mechanics necessary for short turns by demonstrating and then having your students practice a series of pivot slips.

8. C. It will be easier for your students to see the extension which you use to facilitate the edge release in a pivot slip if you demonstrate it *in the vertical direction* (up and down).

9. *Momentarily stops their forward movement, provides a platform from which to move and provides a sense of control.* The edge-set at the bottom of the flexion of each hop turn momentarily stops the forward (downhill) movement. The edge-set will be helpful on steep terrain because it will provide both a platform from which to move and a sense of control.

10. *Friction.* A forward and diagonal sideslip reduces speed because of the friction of the edges scraping across the snow.

11. *To stabilize their body for balance to block the body to keep it from moving forward at the same rate as their skis.* Having your students plant the downhill pole at the same time they set their edges (after sideslipping while maintaining upper and lower body separation) stabilizes the body. This is

necessary not only for balance, but to block the body. Because the body is moving forward at the same rate as the skis, once they set their edges their body will continue to move downhill unless they block it with a solid pole plant.

12. A. If it is necessary to focus on pole use in addition to the edge-set so that your students will have their poles ready when they set their edges, use only the diagonal sideslip and edge-set. Have your students swing the pole forward while progressively flexing in a diagonal sideslip. Then have them drop the pole point into the snow when they set the edges.

13. *False*. A more advanced means of controlling speed on steep terrain is to use a round, finished turn shape instead of pivoting and edge-sets.

     However, pivoting is an important element, because it gives students the ability to control their speed.

14. B. To improve your students' skiing performance on steep terrain, you must create a more balanced application of skills. Round, finished turns are a more advanced means of controlling speed on steep terrain.

     Students will still have to use pivoting in short turns, however, because even the most aggressively-shaped skis are incapable of making a purely carved turn with a radius small enough to control speed on steep terrain.

15. *They will take place together*. It may make sense to your students to think about rolling their feet and ankles before they begin to pivot their skis. In reality, the movements will happen together because the act of tipping the feet into the new turn leads to a rotation of the thigh. Rotating the thighs gives some direction to the skis.

16. A) *Allows it to be absorbed*. Flexing correctly will allow the pressure that builds up on the skis after the fall line to be absorbed.

     B) *They can become overloaded and either bounce, chatter, or rebound*. Without such flexion, the ski will become overloaded and will either bounce and chatter in the snow, or will load so quickly that the resulting rebound will likely cause students to lose their balance and end up with their hips behind their feet. Such a mistake will almost certainly lead to a loss of control.

     C) *Allows them to increase*. Flexion also allows the student to increase the edge angles during the second half of the turn, which means that the skis will continue to bend and help shape the bottom of the turn.

17. B. Teaching students to move the hips across the skis *before* the edges have been released will often lead to a disjointed and poorly-balanced turn entry.

18. *Short medium turn*. Given the steeper terrain, a short medium turn is probably the best radius for the leapers exercise.

19. *Hips are over their feet*. If students have difficulty staying within the corridor in the pivot slips exercise, there could be a stance problem. If necessary, spend a little time to be sure that their hips are over their feet and that they can maintain pressure on the balls and arches of their feet.

Notes

Powder

Lesson Outcome

Students learn to link turns in powder snow. They learn to use unweighting and powerful twisting movements of the feet and legs to overcome the added resistance created by deeper snow. Through the progressions in this chapter, students who have become confident and skillful in powder are able to further improve their performance.

For many people, skiing in deep, ungroomed powder snow is one of the most pleasurable experiences skiing has to offer. The sensation of the skis floating through the snow as the student moves effortlessly down the hill is matched by few other experiences in sports. For others, the mystique of skiing powder is overshadowed by the challenge and intimidation of having their feet and skis "swallowed" by the deep snow.

Introducing powder skiing requires a good plan which involves solid stance and balancing skills, and perhaps above all, patience on your part! Turning in powder snow is shown in photo 9.

Many of the difficulties of powder snow, as well as the delights, are caused by the increased resistance offered by the dense snow. Two approaches can be taken to manage the difficulties. The first is learning to allow a slight increase in speed over normal speeds on packed slopes. This is done to overcome the increased friction from the snow. The second is to weight the skis more equally than on packed slopes. Otherwise, the

Photo 9. Turning in Powder Snow

"light" ski will be deflected by the increased snow resistance, while the "heavy" ski tends to dive.

If you have the opportunity, make sure that your students rent or buy some of the new powder skis. Since they are so wide and buoyant, they make powder and crud skiing significantly easier than it has ever been. Even people in poor physical condition have been able to ski soft, loose snow with ease and without exaggerated techniques, such as leaping and hopping.

These skis should not be considered only as teaching aids or as "cheaters." They are an essential and welcome breakthrough in our quest to teach people to ski in all conditions.

The Warm-up Run

If possible, start the powder lesson with a warm-up run on groomed terrain. Active, short fall-line turns will probably warm the group up more quickly than longer turns. Since most of your students will probably be anxious to get into

powder snow, the quick pace of the warm-up run also helps set the stage for the rest of the lesson. During the warm-up run, draw attention to the elements of a good short turn:

- strong, quiet upper body;
- rhythmic pole swing;
- strong, active twisting (or steering) and tipping (or edging) movements of the feet and legs; and
- flexion and extension.

Discuss short turns with your students and check their understanding. How do they unweight their skis? When do they redirect skis toward the new turn? How do they select turn shape? All of these elements are important in powder skiing.

On groomed snow, even short turns usually have a fairly high degree of finish to help control speed. (This varies depending on slope pitch.) Powder snow presents more frictional resistance against the feet and skis than groomed snow. This friction slows the student down.

Skiing in powder therefore requires that the shape of the turn be a bit less finished so that the student can maintain enough momentum to continue down the hill. A turn that is too finished robs the student of the necessary momentum and makes the initiation of the next turn much more difficult than it needs to be.

Increased friction requires students to apply more power to steer their feet and legs. The timing of the twisting movements is important: many students equate strong steering movements with quick movements. Explain that while they may need to use more power to guide the skis in deep snow, they should apply the movements with patience!

Edging

Edging movements (tipping the feet and legs) are still necessary in powder, but their purpose is not to make the skis bite or hold. The edging movements increase the capacity of the ski to bend and turn. Subtle usage of ankles and knees helps tip the skis onto their edges while keeping them more or less underneath the body, enhancing balance.

Safety Considerations

Before heading into the powder, make the group aware of some of the special safety considerations of skiing in powder snow.

1. Avoid skiing deep powder alone. With a partner, there will always be someone close by in case you fall and cannot get up.
2. Take the pole straps off of your wrists. This will prevent you from being unable to move your arms in a head-first fall in deep snow.
3. Use powder cords to make it easier to find a ski that has re-leased.
4. When teaching in deep snow, you should generally go last so that you are in a position to help a student who has fallen and is either having difficulty getting up or putting a ski back on. This is especially true during longer practice segments. Limit your demonstration length (one or two turns will do) so that you do not get too far from the group. You may want to have the group move down the hill below you so that you will be above or with them most of the time. Skiing toward the group will also make it easier for them to see your demonstration.

Terrain

It is ideal to introduce your students to powder snow on moderate, ungroomed terrain that flattens out onto a groomed slope. Being able to see the transition from the more challenging and perhaps more intimidating deep snow, back to the groomed snow, can have a psychological advantage.

Another option is to use a trail where only one side is groomed. In such a situation, you have the ability to go from groomed snow to powder and back without having to commit (mentally and physically) to an entire run in ungroomed snow. If such a run is available, it provides the luxury of letting students ski in the deep snow as much or as little as they wish. This helps build confidence as well as provide periods of rest during each run.

Bouncing Turns in the Powder: Traverse

By having your students extend and lighten the skis (so-called "up-unweighting") from a traverse, then gradually having them move from garland turns into skiing in the fall line, you will build their confidence and give them skills for skiing powder.

1. From a shallow traverse in deep snow, demonstrate very active flexion and extension. Show good hand position, be sure the flexion and extension movements come from the ankles and knees, and do not break at the waist. Each time you push your skis into the snow, the snow under the skis is compacted. The compacted snow creates a platform under the skis so that the extension movement brings the skis back up and out of the snow.
2. Invite the group to try the same movements, preferably each in their own section of untracked snow.
3. For the next segment, you can continue in the same direction if the terrain allows, or you can turn around and traverse back in the opposite direction. This time, demonstrate even more active flexion/extension movements. The goal is to actually

bounce your feet and skis in and out of the snow.

4. Have the group practice flexing and extending more actively. Point out that each time they bounce up, their feet and skis are closer to the surface of the snow.

    Pay special attention to your students' fore/aft balance. Many students think they should lean back in powder to keep the tips of their skis out of the snow. Point out that when they maintain more even pressure along the length of their feet (and skis), they do not tire as quickly. When they lean back, they have to use the strength of their thighs to hold their bodies up. A more centered stance, on the other hand, allows them to use their strength to twist the feet and skis. Stress that good hand position and a quiet upper body add stability.

5. Have your students repeat this exercise at least a couple of times in each direction, if necessary.

6. If students do not use their poles when they bounce in the traverse, show them how to add a pole plant to each bounce and then have them practice.

Bouncing Traverse: Garlands

When the group can accurately perform the bouncing traverse, have them add twisting movements of the feet and legs. A garland approach eliminates some of the apprehension of trying to make a full turn in deep snow. The goal is to capitalize on active up-unweighting by twisting the feet

toward the fall line. By bouncing up toward the surface of the deep snow, the resistance to steering the skis is reduced. This provides an opportunity to get the feet and skis turning in the desired direction.

1. Demonstrate shallow traverse bounces once again.
2. On roughly the third bounce, plant your pole and twist your feet and skis toward the fall line to start a half-turn.
3. Bounce again, planting your uphill pole, and twist your feet and skis back across the hill.

    Stick to short turn shapes in the garlands to provide a better sense of rhythm and timing.
4. Have your students try this sequence several times in both directions.
5. As the group gains confidence in their ability to turn their skis on demand, demonstrate garlands that go gradually deeper into the fall line before turning back across the hill. Remind students that they do not need to finish their turns as much in deep snow as on a groomed slope.
6. As your group becomes more confident, work this exercise line into linked turns in the fall line. As you add turning to the bouncing, emphasize the need for continuing the rhythm of the bouncing movements. Continue to practice these bouncing turns on subsequent runs. If some students still have difficulty turning their skis with a combination of unweighting and steering, show them how to use the more powerful movement of

twisting with the hips to help turn the feet and skis.

Note: Be aware that you may need to monitor the fitness levels of your group—and potentially, the fatigue levels. If they seem to be getting tired, suggest a rest period, or a couple of runs on groomed terrain to allow recovery.

Converting Up-unweighting to Retraction

After your group has become reasonably proficient with bouncing to up-unweight to initiate a turn, ask them to try pulling their feet toward their hips instead of pushing their feet into the snow to create a platform. The turn rhythm remains the same, but the skis are pulled toward the surface of the snow instead of pushing the body away from the feet. The advantage of this movement is that the legs are bent when the skis are near the snow surface, which provides more power to twist the feet and skis toward the next turn. Be patient, demonstrating frequently so that the group gets a good, clear picture of what you are asking of them.

Extension-Retraction in Deep Snow

An extension-retraction movement pattern helps students ski powder with more style and finesse. This movement pattern is one in which you redirect the extension from a more vertical direction to one that is more lateral. The timing of extension also changes. You no longer use the extension to flatten the skis and up-unweight, but rather to push the skis deeper and somewhat laterally (away from the body) into the snow during the middle of the turn. Since skis are generally wider and softer in the tips and tails than they are under the feet, the resistance of the snow will cause the skis to bend. When skis bend, they form an arc.

As the skis leave the fall line (as the turn continues), you stop pushing against them and use your hip flexors to pull your feet back toward your body. The bend in the skis allows the tips of the skis to come back toward the surface of the snow. This combination of factors leaves your body low and flexed, with your skis at or near the snow surface. While remaining flexed, you roll the ankles and knees toward the next turn (or down the hill).

This movement changes the edges of the skis, and as the legs rotate toward the next turn, helps create a rotary force to start the new turn. Finally, you need to extend laterally again while continuing to twist your feet and legs to once again cause the skis to bend into an arc.

While this series of movements may seem complex, it is actually fairly easy to teach. This is especially true if you teach retraction in the context of relaxation. Instead of actively pulling the legs and feet back toward the body, simply relax the muscles of the legs to utilize the features of the ski. A ski bent in the snow returns to camber as it climbs back toward the surface of the snow. The ability to link bouncing traverses or turns is a prerequi-site for this exercise.

1. In deep snow, demonstrate a very shallow traverse with your legs flexed.
2. Using the inside/uphill leg for balance and support, push the downhill ski down into the snow by extending the downhill leg. The ski begins to bend in the snow.
3. Without standing up, relax the muscles of the downhill leg. The ski comes back to the surface of the snow.
4. Have your students try the same movement. Watch them carefully to be sure that they are using the leg to push the ski into the snow as opposed to flexing in the ankles, knees, and hips and suddenly halting the downward movement. The latter action would push the ski into the snow, but leave the student too flexed to be able to relax the leg without standing up (extending).
5. Once you have made any necessary corrections, have your students repeat this exercise a number of times in each direction.
6. You are now ready to incorporate turning. Demonstrate once again how to push the downhill ski into the snow.
7. Relax the muscles of your downhill leg.
8. When your ski comes back to the surface, plant your pole and twist both your feet and legs toward the new turn while pushing the outside ski into the snow.
9. Have your students try a single turn first in one direction, then the other.
10. Next, have your students link a series of turns.

Choosing a relatively low number of turns as an initial goal will help students who may be apprehensive about the new movements and/or deep snow. Teaching this progression takes little time but having your students practice the movements easily fills the majority of time available in any lesson.

As you gain experience in teaching both of these powder progressions, you may choose to try the second progression first. If it does not create the desired outcome for your students, then try the first progression as your back-up. In general, the latter progression is more suitable for more skillful students, but can be used successfully for new powder skiers.

Variation of the Extension-Retraction Progression

The extension-retraction progression may be taught so that it is more appropriate for lesser skilled or more apprehensive students.

1. From a traverse, demonstrate an up-stem while maintaining some degree of flexion in your overall stance. This means you should step the uphill ski into a wedge stance.
2. Transfer weight to the stemmed ski.

The act of stemming the ski is a steering movement. In essence, you are pre-steering or turning the ski in the intended direction of travel. Once you have transferred weight to the ski, it begins to turn down the hill. Extending against that ski helps make it bend and turn.

3. Plant your pole and relax your inside leg. The inside ski will tend to come parallel with the outside one with very little effort.

4. Have your students try this sequence.

5. Have students repeat the same sequence in the opposite direction, then begin to link turns.

Students should begin to use more active twisting or steering movements of the inside leg as they gain confidence in linking turns. With more practice time, students will soon be able to reduce the stemming action of the new outside ski. Stemming the new ski helps build a sense of control and gives them confidence in their ability to start the next turn in spite of the added resistance of the deep snow.

Be careful not to rush them past the stem initiation too quickly. Students will reduce the use of the stem when they are ready. Be creative and try as many variations of these soft snow progressions as you can come up with. Experiment also with the pacing of the information to see how slowly or quickly you can present it and still have your students assimilate it. The pace depends upon the particular group. Persistence and patience will enable your students to succeed!

Questions: Powder

1. Write either "powder" or "groomed snow" in the space provided next to each of the following statements:
    (Assume a hill of the same pitch and that you want to ski at the same speed)

    A) _____ You need a more finished turn shape to control your speed

    B) _____ More friction

    C) _____ You have to use more power to steer your skis

    D) _____ The purpose of edging movements is to make the skis bite or hold

2. What are three things mentioned in the study guide that you can do to make skiing in powder safer?

    _____

    _____

    _____

3. Circle the best choice:
    When teaching in deep snow, you should generally go (first) / (last), especially during longer practice segments.

4. Circle the best choice:
    In powder, demonstrating going (away from) / (toward) the group will make it easier for them to see what you are doing.

5. Choose one or more of the following:
    On what type(s) of terrain does the study guide suggest introducing your students to powder snow
    A. On moderate ungroomed terrain that flattens out onto a groomed slope
    B. On a trail where one side is groomed and the other is not
    C. Neither of the above

6. Fill in the blank with the name of one or more joints of the body:
    In the first step of the bouncing in a traverse progression, when you demonstrate a very active flexion and extension, you should make sure that the flexion and extension movements come from your

    _____ and that you do not break at the waist.

7. Fill in the blank:
    Each time you push your skis into the snow, the snow under the skis will be compacted.

    The compacted snow will create a _____ under the skis so that the extension movement brings the skis back up and out of the snow.

8. Why is leaning back in powder more tiring than using a centered stance?

_____

9. True or false:
   A good hand position and a quiet upper body add stability when bouncing in a traverse.

10. In a powder garland, how does actively up-unweighting by twisting your feet toward the
    fall line make it easier to steer the skis?

_____

11. Circle the best choice:
    Use fairly (short) / (long) turn shapes in the powder garlands to provide a better sense of rhythm and timing.

12. Fill in the blank with the name of a part or parts of the body:
    Once they have added turning to the bouncing they are doing in the garlands, some students may have
    difficulty turning their skis with a combination of unweighting and steering. Show them how to use the

    more powerful movement of twisting with the _____ to help them turn their feet and skis.

13. Circle the best choice:
    In an extension-retraction turn in the powder, you (use) / (do not use) the extension to flatten
    the skis and up-unweight.

14. Fill in the blank with the name of a type of muscle:

    To retract your legs, you use your hip _____ s.

15. According to the study guide, what advantage does pulling the feet toward the hips (retracting them)
    to initiate a turn in powder have over up-unweighting?

_____

16. Circle the best choice:
    When teaching extension-retraction, watch your students carefully to be sure that they
    (first flex in the ankles, knees, and hips and then powerfully and quickly halt the downward movement /
    (use the leg to push the ski into the snow).

17. Choose the best answer:
    To adapt the extension-retraction progression for lesser skilled or more apprehensive students,
    have them use:
    A.   A down-stem
    B.   An up-stem
    C.   A wide-track parallel

Answers: Powder

1. A=*Groomed snow*, B=*Powder*, C=*Powder*, D=*Groomed snow*. On groomed snow, even short turns usually have a fairly high degree of finish to help control speed (A). In powder snow, however, the shape of the turn will generally be straighter than it would on groomed snow; that is, it will have less finish than the same turn would have on groomed snow. This is because there is more frictional resistance against the feet and skis due to the deep snow (B). This friction will slow the student down. Friction requires you to apply more power to steer your feet and legs. (C). Edging movements (tipping the feet and legs) are still necessary in powder, but their purpose is not to make the skis bite or hold (D). Instead, those movements increase the capacity of the ski to bend and turn. Subtle usage of the ankles and knees helps tip the skis onto their edges while keeping them more or less underneath the body, thereby enhancing balance.

2. *Avoid skiing in deep powder alone. Take the pole straps off of your wrists. Use powder cords.* Some special safety considerations of skiing in powder snow: 1) Avoid skiing in deep powder alone. With a partner, there will always be someone close by in case you fall and cannot get up; 2) Take the pole straps off of your wrists. This will prevent you from being unable to move your arms in a head-first fall in deep snow; 3) Use powder cords to make it easier to find a ski that has released in a fall.

3. *Last.* When teaching in deep snow, you should generally go last so that you are in a position to help a student who has fallen and is either having difficulty getting up or putting a ski back on. This is especially true during longer practice segments. Limit your demonstrations of new movements to one or two turns so that you do not get too far from the group.

4. *Toward.* Demonstrating toward the group will make it easier for them to see what you are doing.

5. A & B. It is probably best to introduce your students to powder snow on moderate ungroomed terrain that flattens out onto a groomed slope. Being able to see the transition from the more challenging and perhaps more intimidating deep snow back to the groomed snow can be psychologically advantageous. Another option is to use a trail where one side is groomed and the other is not. In such a situation, you have the ability to go from groomed snow to powder and back again without having to commit (mentally and physically) to an entire run in ungroomed snow. If such a run is available, it provides the luxury of letting your students ski in the deep snow as much or as little as they wish. This will help build their confidence, as well as provide periods of rest during each run.

6. *Ankles and knees.* When you demonstrate very active flexion and extension from a shallow traverse in deep snow, show good hand position, be sure the flexion and extension movements come from the ankles and knees, and do not break at the waist.

7. *Platform.* Each time you push your skis into the snow, the snow under the skis will be compacted. The compacted snow will create a platform under the skis so that the extension movement brings the skis back up and out of the snow.

8. *You have to use the strength of your thighs to hold your body up.* When you lean back, you have to use the strength of your thighs to hold your body up. A more centered stance, on the other hand, allows you to use your strength to twist your feet and skis.

9.   *True.* A good hand position and a quiet upper body add stability when bouncing in a traverse.

10. *Bounces you up toward the surface of the deep snow, where the resistance to steering the skis is less.* When you actively up-unweight by twisting your feet toward the fall line in a powder garland, you bounce up toward the surface of the deep snow, where the resistance to steering the skis is less.

11. *Short.* Stick to short turn shapes in powder garlands to provide a better sense of rhythm and timing.

12. *Hips.* As your students add turning to the bouncing which they began in the garlands, some of them will have difficulty turning their skis with a combination of unweighting and steering. Show them how to use the more powerful movement of twisting with the hips to help turn the feet and skis.

13. *Do not use.* In an extension-retraction movement pattern, you no longer use the extension to flatten the skis and up-unweight, but rather to push the skis deeper and somewhat laterally (away from the body) into the snow during the middle of the turn.

14. *Flexors.* You use your hip flexors to pull your feet back toward your body.

15. *Legs will be bent when the skis are near the snow's surface, making it easier to twist the feet and skis toward the next turn.* When your group has become reasonably proficient with bouncing to up-unweight to initiate a turn, ask them to try pulling their feet toward their hips instead of pushing them into the snow to create a platform. The advantage of this movement is that the *legs will be bent when the skis are near the snow surface,* which provides more power to twist the feet and skis toward the next turn.

16. *Use the leg to push the ski into the snow.* When teaching extension-retraction, watch your students carefully to be sure that they are using the leg to push the ski into the snow as opposed to flexing in the ankles, knees, and hips and suddenly halting the downward movement. The latter will push the ski into the snow, but will leave the student too flexed to be able to relax the leg without standing up (extending).

17. B. Teach your lesser skilled or more apprehensive students a version of the extension-retraction progression where they use an up-stem.

Notes

Crud

Lesson Outcome

Students learn to adapt the movements used for powder skiing to successfully ski in crud and broken snow. They learn to unweight, and to control the size and shape of turns.

Skiing in crud snow can be quite challenging. Even the name sounds uninviting to most students. Because crud has inherent inconsistencies in its snow surface, balance can present a special challenge of its own. The inconsistency of crud snow can also lead to difficulties in unweighting and directing the skis. Turning in crud snow is shown in photo 10.

You can use many of the same progressions outlined in the chapter on powder to teach students to ski in crud. In fact, as a powder lesson progresses into the afternoon, you may be teaching more in broken or cut-up snow than in uncut, consistent powder. If you are teaching an off-piste lesson days after the last snowfall, it is likely that your group will encounter crud snow. As in many new situations, the primary concern for students is often to link turns so that they feel in control. Initiating turns on a spot that has been skied out is usually not much of a problem. However, initiating turns on an inconsistent snow surface, such as where a pillow of uncut snow still exists, definitely can be problematic for students.

Students who can ski powder have the skills to turn in these crud pillows but may need to develop the ability to see and recognize

Photo 10. Turning in Crud Snow

A

B

transitional snow. Students who have little experience in deep snow need both the skills and the tactics to link turns in powder and to recognize transitional snow.

As noted in the Powder chapter, if you have the opportunity, make sure that your students rent or buy some of the new powder skis. These wide, buoyant skis make crud and powder skiing significantly easier. Even people in poor physical condition have been able

to ski soft and loose snow at ease without exaggerated techniques (such as leaping and hopping). These skis should not be considered only as teaching aids or as "cheaters." They are an essential and welcome breakthrough in our quest to teach people to ski in all conditions.

Hop Turns

Turns utilizing strong unweighting movements are a good place to start. Up-unweighting is the easiest to see and execute. Have your students start with hop turns. These should be done on a groomed slope with a pitch similar to the crud snow run you intend to ski. Demonstrate and then have your group practice hop turns, emphasizing certain points.

- Hop by quickly and powerfully extending in the ankles and knees.
- Face the upper body down the hill and stabilize it with a solid pole plant. One pole should be in the snow at all times.
- Steer the skis by twisting the feet and legs. This steering should not cause the hips to follow where the skis are pointing. Explain that on very steep crud runs, the hop turn may be the best way to get down the hill.

Leapers Progression

With this in mind, while you are still on groomed terrain, lead the group through a series of leapers.

1. Demonstrate a leaper in which

you steer your skis in the air only enough to get the next turn started, instead of hopping and turning the feet far across the hill. For this exercise, use a medium-radius turn.

2. Upon landing, focus on absorbing the impact by flexing the ankles and knees progressively through the rest of the turn. Explain that leapers provide a good means of initiating a turn in the crud because the hop gets the skis out of the snow where they are easy to steer.

3. Have your students practice what you have just shown them.

4. Demonstrate and have your students practice another set of leapers. This time, have the students focus on making powerful steering (twisting) and edging (tipping) movements with their feet and legs during the progressive flexion that takes place after landing. Make them aware that they need to make these movements in the crud because it is often denser than powder snow.

5. Demonstrate a few more leapers, this time changing edges in the air so that you land on a new set of edges.

6. Have your students practice leapers, changing edges in the air. Be sure that they continue to execute the powerful steering and edging movements after they have landed.

7. Once the group can successfully perform the task, have them repeat the exercise, this time shortening the radius of the turn slightly. The shorter radius will provide a better sense of rhythm when skiing in crud.

The important elements of this exercise as it applies to crud are the aggressive up-unweighting (via the hop) and the powerful steering and edging movements after landing to drive the skis through the dense snow.

Using Leapers to Ski Crud Snow

Now that you have prepared the group with this movement pool, you are ready to start skiing in crud. Start the group on a run with tracked or broken snow. Point out how some sections of snow have only a few tracks through them, while others have so many tracks that small parts of the run actually seem to be packed. Explain to your students that in any given run on this trail, they go intermittently from packed to unpacked sections. Therefore, they need a combination of mechanics and tactics that allows them to link consistent turns. In this context, tactics refers to a plan of action that enables them to succeed. For most students, this means choosing a movement pool that works in the deeper snow and maintaining those movements even when initiating a turn on one of the packed spots.

For your students' first attempt in the crud, have them use the leapers you have just taught them. Encourage them to do the leapers exactly as they have practiced them. Demonstrate three or four turns, then be available to provide encouragement and feedback. As in powder, it is important from both a psychological point of view as well as for safety that you do

not get too far away from the group, especially early in the lesson. As the group gains confidence, lengthen the skiing segments.

Pulling the Feet toward the Hips

After a run or two, the group should be ready to expand their pool of movements. Have them replace the push against the feet that creates the hop with a pull of the feet toward the hips. Demonstrate this movement for your students and provide them with plenty of time to practice it.

Pay particular attention to steering, edging, and extension.

• Students should continue to use powerful (but progressive) twisting movements to steer their skis through the crud.

• Students should continue to tip their feet and knees inward. This will help put the skis on edge where they can bend and create part of the turning force (a ski that is tipped on edge will bend into an arc and therefore turn in the snow).

• When students first try to pull the skis toward the hips instead of hopping, they may forget to follow with extension. For the first few attempts, that is acceptable; however, once they begin to pull their feet up to change edges and start the turn, coach them to extend so that the skis are pressed away from the body and into the snow.

This helps apply pressure to the ski so that it can bend. It may be helpful to ask the group to imagine that they are skiing through a cave or low tunnel. If they extend to move the hips up to start the turn, they will hit their heads on the ceiling. Instead, they need to pull their feet up, then roll the ankles and knees downhill to change edges and start the next turn.

Maintaining Rhythmic Pole Swings

Swinging the poles rhythmically makes it easier to initiate turns and adds a sense of rhythm to the turns. Hesitating in the transition between turns makes new turns very difficult to start. Suggest to your students that they try to keep their poles moving; by the time they have planted one pole in the snow, they should already be starting to swing the other forward. Many students need to practice this motion quite a bit be sure to provide adequate practice time and continuously reinforce the correct motion. If you feel your students need additional help timing their pole action, demonstrate it for them on groomed terrain.

1. In a short to short-medium turn, begin to swing your pole forward as you normally would.
2. At the same time, without changing the position of your hand relative to your torso, begin to swing the other pole shaft back to touch the thigh of the inside leg.
3. Try to time the movements so that your pole plant occurs at the same time that the shaft of

your other pole actually touches your thigh.
4. As soon as you have planted your pole, begin to swing the pole (that was touching your thigh) forward.
5. Swing the pole you just planted back toward your thigh. The main goal is to keep both poles moving all the time.

Simultaneous Leg Movements in Crud Snow

As students improve their ability to negotiate crud, begin to emphasize the importance of simultaneous movements of the legs. Tipping and turning both legs at the same time prevents the skis from being pulled in different directions by the inconsistent snow. However, both skis are not equally weighted throughout the turn. The outside ski carries most of the pressure for the majority of the turn, with more equal weighting occurring during the transition from one turn to the next. The inside ski should remain fairly light. Because the lack of pressure on the inside ski makes it more susceptible to being "grabbed" by crud, you need to use muscular effort to tip and actively guide it at the same time and in the same direction as the outside ski. If simply mentioning this idea is not enough to help your students develop their inside leg activity, you can use knee chases on groomed terrain.

Knee Chases

1. Start in the fall line on a gentle slope and demonstrate a half-

turn to a stop. Tip the inside leg so that it leads the outside leg in the intended direction of the turn. The outside knee chases the inside knee, but should not catch it. Keep the inside knee moving into the hill.
2. Have each person try a half-turn to a stop, first in one direction and then in the other. Be sure they keep the inside ski very light, but on the snow. The goal is to tip and turn both legs and skis while keeping the majority of pressure on the outside ski.
3. Once the students can execute the movements correctly, have them practice knee chases by linking a series of turns. This exercise should help develop inside leg activity.

Your students should now be well on their way to becoming competent crud skiers! To help keep them from becoming frustrated, encourage them to be patient, and remind them that there is no substitute for practice and mileage.

Questions: Crud

1. Choose the best answer:
   Which chapter contains many progressions which are also appropriate for crud?
   A. Ice
   B. Powder
   C. Steeps

2. Choose the best answer:
   Which type of unweighting is the easiest to see and execute?
   A. Down-unweighting
   B. Lateral-unweighting
   C. Up-unweighting

3. On what type of pitch and on what type of snow does the study guide suggest introducing hop turns?

   _____

4. Circle the best choice:
   In hop turns, the extension should come from the (ankles and knees) / (hips).

5. Choose one or more of the following:
   In hop turns:
   A. You use your poles to stabilize your upper body
   B. One pole should be in the snow at all times
   C. Neither of the above

6. True or false:
   In hop turns, your hips should follow your skis.

7. Choose one or more of the following:
   To get down a very steep crud run, you probably would not want to use:
   A. Hop turns
   B. Round turns
   C. Step turns

8. Choose the best answer:
   At the beginning of the leapers exercise, you first demonstrate a leaper in which you steer your skis in the air only enough to get the next turn started. For this part of the exercise, you should use more of a:
   A. Short-radius turn
   B. Medium-radius turn
   C. Long-radius turn

9. Fill in the blank with the name of two or more parts of the body:
   In the leapers progression, when you land after leaping, you should focus on absorbing the impact by flexing your _____ progressively through the rest of the turn.

10. Why are leapers a good means of initiating turns in the crud?

_____

11. Circle the best choice:
You need to use (powerful) / (subtle) twisting and tipping movements with your feet and legs in the crud because crud is often denser than powder snow.

12. Fill in the blank with one or more words:
Once you have given your students some time to try out leapers in the crud, have them replace the push against the feet that creates the hop with _____.

13. In which exercise or progression does the study guide suggest using the cave or tunnel image and why?

_____

_____

14. Fill in the blank with the name of a part of the body:
To help your students maintain a good rhythm by keeping their poles constantly moving, you can have them swing one pole forward while beginning to swing the other back toward the adjacent

_____ .

15. Circle the best choice:
To prevent the skis from being pulled in different directions by inconsistent snow, tip and turn them (sequentially) / (simultaneously).

16. Circle the best choice:
When skiing the crud, your skis (will) / (will not) be equally weighted throughout the turn.

17. Which ski is more susceptible to being grabbed by the crud and why?

_____

18. Circle the best choice:
Knee chases can help your students learn to use muscular effort to tip and actively guide their skis (simultaneously) / (sequentially).

19. Choose one or more of the following:
You often teach students to actively pull their feet and legs back toward the body (by contracting the hip flexors) for skiing:
A. Crud
B. Powder
C. Steeps

Answers: Crud

1. B. You can use many of the same progressions outlined in the chapter on powder to teach students to ski in crud.

2. C. *Up-unweighting* is the easiest type of unweighting to see and execute.

3. *On a groomed slope with a pitch similar to the crud run you intend to ski.* Have your students try some hop turns on a groomed slope with a pitch similar to the crud run you intend to ski.

4. *Ankles and knees.* In hop turns, you hop by quickly and powerfully extending in the ankles and knees.

5. A & B. In hop turns, you face the upper body down the hill, and stabilize it with a solid pole plant. One pole should be in the snow at all times.

6. *False.* In hop turns, you steer the skis by twisting the feet and legs. This steering should not cause the hips to follow where the skis are pointing.

7. C. On very steep crud runs, you probably would not want to use step turns. Hop turns may be the best way to get down the hill on such types of runs. A rounder turn shape, however, is more desirable.

8. B. At the beginning of the leapers progression, you first demonstrate a leaper in which you steer your skis in the air only enough to get the next turn started. For this part of the exercise, you should use more of a *medium-radius turn.*

9. *Ankles and knees.* In the leapers progression, when you land after leaping, you should focus on absorbing the impact by flexing the *ankles and knees* progressively through the rest of the turn.

10. *Because they get the skis out of the snow where they are easy to steer.* Leapers provide a good means of initiating a turn in the crud because the hop gets the skis out of the snow where they are easy to steer.

11. *Powerful.* You need to make powerful steering (twisting) and edging (tipping) movements with your feet and legs in the crud because crud is often denser than powder snow.

12. *A pull of the feet toward the hips (or retraction).* Once you have given you students some time to try out leapers in the crud, have them replace the push against the feet that creates the hop with a pull of the feet toward the hips.

13. *Leapers to make sure they don't extend vertically.* You use the cave or tunnel image in the part of the *leapers progression* where you teach students to pull their feet toward their hips. It helps them focus on extending their skis *away* from the body. You ask the group to imagine that they are skiing through a cave or low tunnel. If they extend to move the hips up to start the turn, they will hit their heads on the ceiling. Instead, they need to pull their feet up, then roll the ankles and knees downhill to change edges and start the next turn.

14. *Thigh.* To help your students maintain a good rhythm by keeping their poles constantly moving, you can have them swing one pole forward while beginning to swing the other back toward the adjacent *thigh.* Have them try to time the movements so that the pole plant occurs at the same time that the shaft of the other pole actually touches the thigh.

15. *Simultaneously.* Tipping and turning both legs at the same time will prevent the skis from being pulled in different directions by inconsistent snow.

16. *Will not.* When skiing the crud both skis will not be equally weighted throughout the turn. The outside ski will carry most of the pressure for the majority of the turn, with more equal weighting occurring during the transition from one turn to the next. The inside ski should remain fairly light.

17. *The inside ski because of lack of pressure on it.* Because the lack of pressure on the inside ski makes it more susceptible to being grabbed by the crud, you need to use muscular effort to tip and actively guide it at the same time and in the same direction as the outside ski.

18. *Simultaneously.* Knee chases can help your students learn to use muscular effort to tip and actively guide the inside ski at the same time and in the same direction as the outside ski. Knee chases focus on tipping and turning both legs and skis while keeping the majority of pressure on the outside ski. They also develop activity of the inside leg.

19. A & B. In powder or crud, you often have students actively pull their feet and legs back toward the body (by contracting the hip flexors). For steeps, the flexion is more *passive,* allowing the pressure of the snow against the bottom of the skis to help push the legs into a more flexed position. By yielding to the pressure, the student absorbs the pressure.

Notes

Ice

Lesson Outcome

Students develop the subtle movements necessary to control their skis on ice. Pressure control is a priority, as are careful rotary movements. Edging movements become progressive to prevent overloading the skis. This helps to prevent chattering and skidding of the skis. Students first learn to create a solid platform, which is a stable base from which the skier can move to initiate a new turn. Later, students learn to soften their movements and subtly blend skills.

With practice time, most students begin to feel considerably more comfortable within a relatively short time. As they increase confidence, they learn to blend edging and pressure-control skills. There are infinite combinations of skill blends, each useful for a specific situation. For example, at higher speeds, the skier is able to use pressure more beneficially and subtly reduce emphasis on rotary skills.

Every skier must learn to deal with ice. Skiers at Western resorts often consider hard-packed winter snow to be ice, but ice is considerably harder and slicker than the hard, chalky snow common to Western areas of low humidity and high elevation. For students, however, both types of snow present a similar challenge: how to make the skis hold and work on hard, icy conditions.

Many skiers try to edge the skis more aggressively in icy condi-

Photo 11. Turning on Hard or Icy Snow

tions. Typically, this only makes the skis slip even more. Others give up on trying to make their skis hold at all and substitute twisting or pivoting movements in an effort to get the skis to go where they want. Still others attempt to bear down on the skis to make them hold. Unfortunately, none of those tactics work particularly well.

Fortunately, most upper-level skiers already possess the skills they need to succeed on ice. They need only learn to apply the skills appropriately. Turning on hard or icy snow is depicted in photo 11.

Note: To ski well in icy conditions, skis must be perfectly tuned. There is no substitute for sharpened edges, enabling the skis to grip and handle well in hard snow and ice.

Creating a Sense of Control

Giving students a means of creating a platform at the bottom of the turn will go a long way toward creating

a sense of control. An aggressive edge-set can be used to momentarily stop the forward and/or lateral movements of the ski. While the final goal is to keep skis moving smoothly from one turn to the next, the creation of this platform gives an added sense of control in icy conditions. Once students know this way to control their speed and link turns together, they are more willing to try more subtle approaches to skiing on icy snow.

Check-hop Garlands

Teach skiers to create a platform via check-hop garlands. As the name implies, you check (or slow) the forward movement of the skis by setting the edges quickly and aggressively. You then make a small hop during which you turn the skis in the air to initiate a half-turn down the hill. This half-turn is used simply to position you for another pivot and edge-set. The entire maneuver is executed like a garland.

1. From a static relationship, demonstrate how to quickly tip the feet and knees into the hill. At the same time, you should flex and plant your pole.

2. Glide for a few ski lengths at a shallow angle to the slope, then twist your skis across the hill while aggressively tipping them onto their edges. Flex your ankles and knees to facilitate both the tipping and twisting movements.

3. As you stop flexing, the edges bite into the ice and the skis stop for a brief moment. You must make a solid pole plant in addition to the edge-set to prevent the upper body from continuing forward and down the hill.

4. From the platform created by the edge-set, extend the ankles and knees quickly and powerfully enough to hop off the snow. The pole you planted aids your stability and balance.

5. While your skis are in the air, twist your feet and legs toward the fall line to get the skis pointing more downhill. You only need to twist the skis enough to get moving diagonally again.

6. Repeat the maneuver three or four times before demonstrating it in the opposite direction.

7. Work this aggressive edge-set (accompanied by a pole plant) into the finish of a short-radius turn. Instead of hopping off the snow to start the next turn, use extension to release the edges and steer the skis into the new turn. (Short-radius turns help students keep the speed down and give most of them more confidence on ice.)

Pumpers

You can use an exercise called pumpers to experiment with skill blends for skiing ice.

Start at the edge of the trail.

1. Statically demonstrate the same basic movement you used to execute the edge-set in the previous progression: flex the downhill knee and ankle forward, and in toward the hill. Point out how the ski is tipped up onto a higher edge during this movement.

   Highlight the fact that the hips and shoulders remain over the downhill ski. This keeps the pressure directly over the edge of the ski, making it bite into the icy snow. Emphasize the need to keep both hands forward as the ski is tipped and its edge engaged.

2. Have the group try this combination of tipping and flexing from a stationary position.

   Point out that once you make the movement, you release it by extending again each time. Once you are satisfied with the basic movement, release it quickly.

3. Each flex and tip of the leg constitutes a pump. Explain that each time the ski is pumped, it bends and bites into the snow. The increased edge angle allows the ski to bend a little more than it would without the tipping movement.

   As it bends, it also turns a little more without stopping in the snow (as it did when checked).

As soon as you pump the ski, release it by extending slightly.

4. Ask the students to execute three pumps during the course of one medium-radius turn one at the top of the turn, another in the fall line, and the third to finish the turn.

   As they release the third pump, they should transfer weight to the other foot and initiate another turn.

5. Have them repeat the three pumps during each of the next few turns.

During a brief stop, ask the group what they felt when they pumped the ski. If the movements were properly done, they will tell you that the ski turned a little more each time they flexed and tipped it.

The flexion and extension movements necessary to create the pumps are important for developing controlled movements on icy snow. Active, yet controlled steering is built into this exercise because skiers must continue to guide the skis in-between pumps to make medium-radius turns.

6. To further improve your group's blend of twisting and tipping movements while skiing on ice, continue with the same exercise line by reducing the number of pumps to two during each turn: one just before the fall line and another to finish.

7. Once the group is comfortable with two pumps, ask them to make only one pump during the last third of each turn. At this point, they must change the timing of the pump itself. Instead

of pumping the ski quickly, they should execute the same movement much more slowly and deliberately.

Try to make the pumping movement last throughout the last third of the turn, while continuing to guide the skis in the intended direction.

Using this progression helps create an active, controlled blend of steering (twisting movements) and edging (tipping movements) while flexing and extending subtly enough to keep the skis from chattering excessively or from skidding out during the turn. As long as the terrain is not overly steep, practice until the students can make well-controlled, medium-radius turns.

This exercise creates a moving platform. By increasing the edge grip of the ski while it continues forward in the snow, there is less potential for interruptions to the student's balance.

Working Pumpers Into Short Turns

Once the students become comfortable with medium turns, you can develop similar subtleties and skill blends in short turns by using the same basic progression.

1. Repeat the static portion of the pumper exercise.
2. Use the pump in a short turn by steering during the top portion of the turn. As the turn nears its completion, pump the ski quickly and powerfully. You should accompany this movement by a solid pole plant, which requires swinging the pole before the pumping movement begins.
3. Release the edge of the ski by rolling the ankles and knees toward the new turn while extending and steering.
4. Repeat this sequence for the next turn.

Practicing this exercise in short turns enables the group to make short-radius turns without "checking" the edges. The outside ski holds better and longer when it continues to move forward in the snow. Having your students practice this exercise until they can do it correctly is important. The more time you allot for practice with the group, the better.

5. As the group becomes more confident, ask them to begin to soften the finish of the turn. They accomplish this by executing the pump of the outside ski less intensely. To keep both skis turning and moving forward in the snow, they should continue to actively guide both skis through the bottom of the turn.

With plenty of practice and encouragement, skiers learn to blend the movements of twisting and tipping the feet and legs while flexing over the outside ski. The subtle combination of these movements, combined with good hand position and pole swing, allows them to ski with relative comfort and confidence in hard, icy conditions.

Conclusion

Be careful not to rush students through the development of the movements outlined in the previously suggested progressions. Spend as much time as necessary to develop each element. Move on *only* when skiers demonstrate competence in the movements and exercises. The process of learning and improving is enjoyable for both you and your students when you can show them how to apply what they can already do to a new or different skiing situation.

Questions: Ice

1. What usually happens when students rely solely upon an aggressive edging movement to control their skis on ice?

    _____

2. What is a check-hop garland?

    _____

    _____

3. Fill in the blank:
    In check-hop garlands, students learn to create a _____ (a stable base from which to initiate a new turn).

4. In a check-hop garland, what can you do to prevent the upper body from continuing forward and down the hill after setting your edges?

    _____

5. Circle the best choice:
    (Check-hop garlands) / (Pumpers) blend the skills of edging and pressure control more harmoniously with steering movements.

6. In pumpers, what is the effect upon your skis' edges when you keep your hips and shoulders over your downhill ski (while tipping and flexing your legs)?

    _____

7. What movements of the leg constitute a "pump" in pumpers?

    _____

8. Choose one or more of the following:
    Tipping the leg in a pumper helps:
    A.   Increase edge angles
    B.   The ski bend more
    C.   The ski turn more

9. True or false:
    The goal of the pumpers exercise is to create a moving platform. By increasing the edge grip of the ski while it continues forward in the snow, there is less potential for interruptions to balance.

10. Originally, during the pumpers progression for medium-radius turns, you ask students to make three pumps. You later ask them to make two, and then only one. At what point(s) in the turn do they make these pumps?

A)   Three pumps: _____

B)   Two pumps: _____

C)   One pump: _____

11. In the pumpers progression, when you reduce the number of pumps to one per turn. Through how much of the turn should you make the pump last?

_____

12. Choose the best answer:
In the pumpers progression for short turns, you should swing your pole:
A.   Before you execute the pump
B.   While you are executing the pump
C.   After you execute the pump

13. Circle the best choice:
As the group becomes more confident in their ability to execute pumpers in short turns,
ask them to "pump" the outside ski (less) / (more) intensely.

Answers: Ice

1. *This only makes the skis slip even more.* Typically, trying to edge the skis more aggressively on slick snow causes them to slip even more.

2. *An exercise where you check the forward movement of the skis by setting your edges quickly and aggressively and then initiate a half turn down the hill by hopping and turning your skis in the air.* Check-hop garlands is an exercise in which you first check (or slow) the forward movement of your skis by setting your edges quickly and aggressively. You then make a small hop during which you turn the skis in the air to initiate a half-turn down the hill. You use this half-turn simply to position yourself for another pivot and edge-set.

3. *Platform.* Teach skiers to create a *platform* through check-hop garlands. A *platform* is a stable base from which the skier can move to initiate a new turn.

4. *Make a solid pole plant.* In a check-hop garland, you must *make a solid pole plant* to prevent the upper body from continuing forward and down the hill.

5. *Pumpers. Pumpers* blend the skills of edging and pressure control more harmoniously with steering movements.

6. *They will bite into the snow.* In pumpers, highlight the fact that the hips and shoulders remain over the down-hill ski. This will keep the pressure directly over the edge of the ski, making it *bite into the icy snow.* Emphasize the need to keep both hands forward as the ski is tipped and its edge engaged.

7. *Each flex and tip* of the leg constitutes a "pump" in pumpers.

8. A, B, & C. By tipping your leg in pumpers, you increase the edge angle of the ski, allowing the ski to bend a little more than it otherwise would. As it bends, it will also turn a little more without stopping in the snow (as it did when checked).

9. *True.* The goal of the pumpers exercise is to create a moving platform. By increasing the edge grip of the ski while it continues forward in the snow, there is less potential for interruptions to balance.

10. A) *One at the top of the turn, one in the fall line, and one at the finish of the turn.* B) *One just before the fall line and another to finish.* C) *During the last third of each turn.*
    During the pumpers progression for medium-radius turns, you execute "pumps" at the following points of the turn: (A) When you make three pumps, you make one at the top of the turn, one in the fall line, and one at the finish of the turn. (B) When you make two pumps, you make one just before the fall line and another to finish. (C) When you make only one pump, you make that during the last third of each turn.

11. *The last third of the turn.* When making only one pump, you change the timing of the pump itself. Instead of pumping the ski quickly, you execute the same movement much more slowly but deliberately. Try to make the pumping movement last throughout the *last third of the turn* while continuing to guide the skis in the intended direction.

12. A. During the pumpers progression for short turns, as the turn nears its completion, pump the ski quickly and powerfully. You should accompany this movement by a solid pole plant, which will require swinging the pole before the pumping movement begins.

13. *Less.* As the group becomes more confident with their ability to execute pumpers in short turns, ask them to begin to soften the finish of the turn. They accomplish this by executing the pump of the outside ski less intensely. To keep both skis turning and moving forward in the snow, they should continue to actively guide both skis through the bottom of the turn.

Notes